China's Brain Drain to the United States

To our wives,
Wu Kaifen and Joy P. Zweig,
for their patience and support

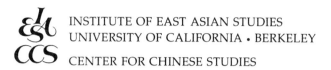

INSTITUTE OF EAST ASIAN STUDIES
UNIVERSITY OF CALIFORNIA • BERKELEY
CENTER FOR CHINESE STUDIES

China's Brain Drain to the United States

Views of Overseas Chinese Students
and Scholars in the 1990s

DAVID ZWEIG and CHEN CHANGGUI
with the assistance of STANLEY ROSEN

A publication of the Institute of East Asian Studies, University of California, Berkeley. Although the Institute of East Asian Studies is responsible for the selection and acceptance of manuscripts in this series, responsibility for the opinions expressed and for the accuracy of statements rests with their authors.

Correspondence may be sent to:
Ms. Joanne Sandstrom, Managing Editor
Institute of East Asian Studies
University of California
Berkeley, California 94720-2318
E-mail: easia@uclink.berkeley.edu

The China Research Monograph series, whose first title appeared in 1967, is one of several publications series sponsored by the Institute of East Asian Studies in conjunction with its constituent units. The others include the Japan Research Monograph series, the Korea Research Monograph series, the Indochina Research Monograph series, and the Research Papers and Policy Studies series. A list of recent publications appears at the back of the book.

Library of Congress Cataloging-in-Publication Data

Zweig, David.
    China's brain drain to the United States : views of overseas
Chinese students and scholars in the 1990s / David Zweig and
Changgui Chen.
        p.   cm. — (China research monograph ; 47)
    Includes bibliographical references.
    ISBN 1-55729-049-0
    1. Chinese students—United States—Attitudes. 2. Chinese
students—United States—Interviews. 3. Scholars—United States—
Attitudes 4. Scholars—United States—Interviews. 5. Brain
drain—China.   I. Chen, Changgui. II. Title. III. Series: China
research monographs ; no. 47.
LC3071.Z84 1995
378.1'9829951073—dc20   95-8737
                                              CIP

Contents

Tables

Figures

Acknowledgments

Professors Chen and Zweig owe an enormous number of debts to many people, most particularly to Peter Harris of the Ford Foundation, which supported our research, and to Professor Stanley Rosen, who organized the California data collection and gave us many insightful comments on the questionnaire. Without the help of Professor Yue Xiaodong, who arranged all the interviews in Boston, as well as Xu Yu, Li Guiting, and Xiao Dong, who arranged interviews in Buffalo, Albuquerque, and New York respectively, we would not have been able to find the people we interviewed. Adam Segal and John Auerbach, Fletcher graduate students, helped us enter the data into the computer and analyze them, while Durwood Marshal of the Tufts Computer Center was a key adviser on methodological aspects of this project. He also ran the multivariate data analysis for us. Research assistance was supplied by Zachary Abuza. Professor Zweig's former student, Shu Yuan, helped with translations. Zhang Lihui and Brent Fulton drove up and down the California coast to carry out our interviews there. An especially large thanks is due to Kevin Kramer, whose wise counsel on many aspects of data collection and analysis was critical to the success of this project, and to his wife, Laura Hettleman, who helped us enter some of the data as well.

At the Fletcher School we received yeoman administrative support from Karin Shirer, who had to handle all the complex financial issues of the grant; Maria Judge, who authorized the financial aspects of the grant; and Professor Zweig's former secretary, Donna Antonucci, who managed the administrative side of Professor Chen's life for him while he was in the United States. In China we appreciate the support of Vice-President and Professor Yao Qihe of Huazhong University of Science and Technology, in Wuhan, who, as Professor Chen's director in the Research Centre on Higher Education, supported our research (both in the United States and in China) and allowed Professor Chen to stay away from his important tasks back in China. With Chen gone, Vice-President Yao's burdens at the center increased enormously. Also, we want to thank Professor Wen Fuxiang, dean of the College of Social Sciences at Huazhong University. We also appreciate the help of Professor Ruth Hayhoe of the Ontario Institute of Studies in Education, in Toronto, and the Canadian

International Development Agency, which supported Professor Chen during his time in Toronto.

Thanks to Professor Tom Gold, who was chair of the Center for Chinese Studies at Berkeley when our study was accepted for publication, and Professor Wen-hsin Yeh, who was chair during the time we revised the manuscript and worked it into shape for publication. A special thanks to Joanne Sandstrom, who is the editor for this book at the Institute of East Asian Studies. Also a special thanks to Kyna Rubin, who gave our manuscript its most extensive review and comments.

Most of all, we owe a great debt to the 273 people who shared their time, their views, and their hopes for a better China with us. It was a difficult decision for them to agree to talk with us. But without their trust and support, this study would have been impossible. We hope that we have not abused that trust in this study and in the manner and tone in which we have presented our findings. We all in our own ways hope that China will soon become the type of society that will be able to draw back its people of talent who went abroad to find a better life.

In the end, we alone are responsible for the content of this study. We spent many hours debating our different perceptions of what the brain drain is all about, what were its causes, and which government was most responsible for its emergence and growth. In the end, we came up with the best solution: use social science methodology to seek the truth, whatever it may be, and then report the findings in as unbiased a way as possible. That is what true collaborative social science is all about, and that is what true friendship across cultural chasms is all about.

Nevertheless, one final note of caution. Before Chen left the United States in October 1993, he wrote a preliminary draft in Chinese. Zweig borrowed readily from that draft, and from the many hours of discussion he and Chen had together, in composing the English manuscript; but in the end, Zweig wrote this manuscript, and primarily for a Western audience. Chen then made general comments on the English draft, which Zweig then revised. Chen did not see the final draft that was submitted. While Zweig understands the need to be sensitive to the Chinese context in which this manuscript will be read, he also recognizes that, at times, in certain instances, his own views may have come out too strongly, and that these views may not totally reflect Chen's own perspectives. Zweig hopes that friends in China will understand the process by which the manuscript was composed.

Summary of the Study

Beginning in 1979, the government of the People's Republic of China, hoping to catch up with Western science and technology, decided for the first time since 1949 to send large numbers of students and scholars to the West to study. While significant numbers of people returned before 1986, after 1987 the ratio of returnees to those leaving dropped significantly. After the June 4, 1989, Tiananmen incident and the U.S. government's decision to allow any mainland Chinese who was then in the United States to apply for permanent residency, the probability that people would return dropped even more precipitously.

Suddenly China found itself in the same situation as many developing countries: sending their "best and brightest" to the United States triggered a "brain drain," and with it the threat that the strategy of sending people abroad to catch up might backfire. But will these people return? If China gets richer and remains politically stable, will the brain drain reverse itself? Which Chinese are most likely to return? What are the current conditions of these students and scholars in the United States? Are they helping their country of origin by working closely with colleagues in China? What are the key issues leading them to stay abroad? What is the real cost of this brain drain? And what policies are most likely to help bring them back?

To answer these and other questions, between January and October 1993, Professors David Zweig and Chen Changgui, with the support of Professor Stanley Rosen and the financial support of the Ford Foundation, carried out 273 interviews with Chinese students, scholars, and other former residents of the People's Republic of China who are currently residing in the United States. The interviews had a wide geographical distribution within the United States, taking place in Boston, New York, Buffalo, Albuquerque, and several centers in California, including Los Angeles, San Diego, and San Francisco. The interviews involved one-on-one meetings that lasted an average of an hour and a quarter and followed a 105-question interview protocol that had been pretested in Toronto in fall 1992.

To make the sample as representative as possible we obtained lists, whenever possible, of Chinese students at a university, and then used a stratified random sample technique in an effort to ensure the randomness of our sample. For visiting scholars we relied mostly on personal contacts, but for people in the workforce, we used a "snowball" sampling technique, collecting lists of names from Chinese we knew, building one big list, and then choosing randomly from that list. To analyze the data we employed both bivariate and multivariate analysis.

While we cannot guarantee that our findings truly reflect the views of the entire population of Chinese students, scholars, and other mainlanders now in the workforce, we have been judicious in our efforts to gain an unbiased cross section of the population we set out to study. We hope that we have been able to reflect their views fairly and accurately.

Key Findings

Patterns of exit. A very high percentage of our sample were the children of intellectuals (52.2 percent) or of high- (5.9 percent) and middle-level cadres (18.5 percent), a finding that suggests that these groups have unequal access to channels out of China. A very large percentage of our sample came from Beijing (43.6 percent) and Shanghai (17.9 percent), suggesting that these two cities control the greatest number of exit channels.

Intentions about returning upon leaving China (figure 5). A significant percentage of our population admitted that when they left China they either had planned not to return (7.5 percent) or were not certain that they would (i.e., were not necessarily planning to return; 40.9 percent). These views about returning were the best predictor of their current plans.

Economic conditions of our U.S. interviewees. We had hypothesized that if the economic conditions of Chinese students and scholars in the United States were relatively good, people would have less incentive to return. We found that the Chinese students and scholars we interviewed were doing quite well in the United States in terms of standard of living. Some 46.7 percent of the sample made more than US$20,000/year (total household income). The mean household income was $20–25,000 (this includes the many "households" that were a single person). Given that we carried out our study when the U.S. economy was emerging from recession, this finding suggests that economic deprivation here is unlikely to make people more interested in returning. Figure 2 illustrates the distribution of income levels among our sample.

Housing in the United States (figure 3). Housing for the sample is not as good as their incomes might indicate—suggesting that many people are saving money by economizing on housing expenses—with the majority of people living in one-bedroom apartments or housing of lesser quality. Nevertheless, 7.7 percent of the sample owned their own housing, and 22.6 percent had a two-bedroom apartment, a statistic that may explain why people with children do not want to go back to China.

Views about returning (see table 1 and figure 4). Of the 267 people who responded to this question, 8.3 percent said they were returning immediately to China, 24.4 percent said that they were definitely returning but did not know when, 19.9 percent were probably going to return and had maintained close ties with China, 19.9 percent were unsure whether they would return, 9.8 percent were probably going to return but had no real links with China, 10.2 percent were unlikely to return unless some major changes occurred in China, and 7.5 percent said they would definitely not return.

Reasons for not returning (tables 3 and 7). When we asked the interviewees to choose from a list of reasons why they might not return, the most common answer was "political instability" (30.3 percent). Other than "political freedom" (12.4 percent), important reasons included factors related to personal development, such as lack of career advancement opportunities (11.6 percent), poor work environment (8.4 percent), limited job mobility (6.0 percent), lack of modern equipment (5.6 percent), and a living standard that was too low (7.6 percent).

The effect of the sex of the respondent. Other than people's "intentions about returning" at the time they left China, the sex of the respondent is usually the best predictor of attitudes about returning among people with children. For a range of reasons—including that women view their possibilities for personal development in China much less optimistically than do men—women are much less likely than men to be planning to go back (25.4 percent of women indicated that they would stay in the United States, as opposed to 14.3 percent of men).

The role of children. Whether or not people had children affected their reasons for returning. The most significant reason that people with children did not want to return to China was the poor housing conditions in China; for people without children, the most important reasons for not returning were household family income in the United States and their comparison of their standard of living in the United States and China. The two groups also differed in the weight they assigned to political factors, those without children picking political factors as reasons for not returning more often than those who had children. We found a statistically significant relationship between people without children who chose

political instability or lack of political freedom as reasons for not returning and their attitudes about returning. For people with children, there
was no clear relationship between concerns about political stability and
views about returning, no doubt because many other concerns went into
their calculations. However, when politics was measured in an alterna-
tive manner, it became clear that politics did affect the decision of people with children.

Family ties. While a significant number of parents did not want their
children to return (41.5 percent), parental views had almost no effect at
all on most people's decisions about returning. Conversely, whether or
not the spouse had joined the interviewee in the United States had a
major effect on people's views about returning.

Political versus economic factors. One of the key issues debated
within the Chinese community is whether the political nature of the
Chinese government or China's low level of economic development best
explains the brain drain. We found that both economic and political factors affect people's decisions about returning. Despite the importance of
economic reasons in our findings, various political concerns, particularly
concerns about political instability, played a significant role in explaining
who was planning to return and who was not. Other political concerns
included suffering during the Cultural Revolution, people's views of the
Tiananmen incident, or mistrust of government policies allowing people
to come and go freely from China. Over 49 percent of the respondents
were uncertain or did not trust that the Chinese government would keep
its word about allowing people who returned to go out of China freely in
the future.

Links to China. We believed that despite a low return rate, we could
argue that the extent of loss due to the brain drain was less if significant
numbers of people maintained contact with their units in China. Half
our sample (50.9 percent) was sending money back to family members
or giving other forms of financial support, while another 18.7 percent
was helping family members come to the United States. A significant
number of people (21.4 percent) were sending back research data to their
home units, while another 18.4 percent were helping other people in their
units come overseas. Also, 24.7 percent of long-term sojourners had
regular contact (three or more times a year) with their home units. Yet
many people (37.7 percent) now had no contact or had never had contact
with their home units, while another 29.1 percent had contact only once
a year, which may simply have been a New Year's card. These findings
suggest that the cost of the brain drain is quite high, although these
scholars are a conduit for the transfer of information back to China.

Ability to change visas. Despite the increase in the number of J-1 student visas issued in the late 1980s as a way to force young university lecturers to return to China after completing their studies, a significant number of people on J-1 visiting scholar visas (29/51) and on J-1 student visas (30/66) had been able to shift their visa status as a result of President Bush's executive order of April 1990. Yet even people on J-1 visiting scholar visas who came after April 1990 have been able to change their status because the Chinese embassy has not been opposing such requests.

Reasons for returning (tables 2 and 6). The most common reasons given for returning were "higher social status in China" (26.0 percent), "better career opportunities in China" (20.5 percent), and "patriotism" (17.3 percent). The things people disliked the most about the United States—the "pace of life too fast" (31.1 percent), crime and personal insecurity (29.2 percent), and lack of job stability (17.2 percent)—could also be reasons people might return.

The role of U.S. government policy. While the number of people returning to China had dropped significantly by the late 1980s, the U.S. government's decision to give permanent residence status to all PRC citizens who were in the United States before April 1990 had a major effect on peoples' views about returning. Among our sample, those people with children who were in the United States before April 1990 were much less likely to be planning to return than those who came after April 1990. In all our multivariate analyses, this was a significant factor. Although we asked only about intentions, and therefore cannot say whether or not this policy will have an effect on behavior, those who came to the United States after April 1990 are much more likely to believe that they will be returning to China.

The effect of "political culture." We had hypothesized that people left and would not return because of what we saw as the "political culture" of the *danwei* (work unit) system in China, which imposes enormous difficulties or constraints on people's lives. We had to reject that hypothesis when people told us that they had relatively good ties with their direct boss and with the co-workers in their work units in China. Women, however, felt more constrained than men by their units, and people did feel constrained by the lack of job mobility and limited opportunities for advancement, which are part of the work unit system in China.

Our multivariate analysis (tables 8–11). Using multivariate analysis, we found a significant difference between the views of people with and without children (see tables 8–11). As mentioned above, people with children were most influenced by housing in the United States, somewhat by politics, while people without children cared most about incomes and living standards, as well as some political factors. Our multivariate analysis also confirmed some of the findings mentioned above.

Strategies for bringing people home. It will not be easy to persuade people to return. Many people do not trust the government's promise that they will be allowed to leave again if they go back. Also, while studies of the brain drain suggest that it is important for work units in the home country to keep contact with people overseas, our data suggest that there is no relationship between links with one's home unit and one's willingness to return. Also, because people fear political instability most, we must question those who assert that political change is a prerequisite for bringing people home, as the transition from an authoritarian regime to a democratic one is likely to trigger a level of instability that will keep most people away.[1] While there is no "quick fix" or one strategy that will reverse the brain drain, an activist government strategy that creates a positive climate for returned scholars and is implemented by a strong leader (in a Park Chung-hee model) or ministry is a necessary step. However, China's institutionalized mistrust of overseas scholars undermines its ability to attract returnees in a way that neither Korea nor Taiwan has had to confront.

Conclusion. Almost 33 percent of our sample are either returning or say that they will definitely return. This finding demonstrates a strong concern for China's future among a large number of Chinese studying in America. Given the importance attributed to economic factors and the fear of political instability, significant numbers of Chinese may return if China successfully weathers Deng Xiaoping's succession and if the economy continues to reform and grow. However, many people in our second category, "definitely will return but don't know when," may be thinking of returning only in the more distant future. The experience of Taiwan and Korea may be relevant in that people studying abroad did not return to those countries until the economies improved significantly and that even then, it took proactive governments to give people strong incentives to uproot themselves from their comfortable living conditions in the United States. Maintaining growth, reform, and stability in China, a country of a billion people, will be no easy task.

---

[1] Zweig would assert that if a stable democracy could be established, more people might return; and he also believes that the current authoritarian strategy may breed its own pattern of instability.

Introduction

Beginning in the late 1970s, China's leaders made a strategic decision to send Chinese scholars overseas for academic and scientific training. The goal was to make up for the years lost through the Cultural Revolution and through these exchanges to catapult China into the top ranks of the global scientific community. While it was not difficult to find Chinese scholars who were interested in going abroad, the critical component of that strategy was to get people to return. In the earlier years of the "open policy in education," the return rate was high. By sending primarily advanced or mature scholars, with established careers and families in China, universities and research labs gained extraordinary benefits from these educational exchanges. However, as the 1980s wore on, fewer and fewer Chinese academics returned. Then came June 4, 1989, and the events in Beijing and in Tiananmen Square, which significantly transformed the "brain drain" into a veritable flood. Many Western governments, responding to demands expressed by the Chinese students and scholars in their communities and to the howls of protest by Chinese communities within their societies, decided to allow Chinese students and scholars to stay for an extended period within their midst and over time have introduced a variety of mechanisms that have allowed those Chinese to stay. As a result, almost 50,000 Chinese students and scholars will stay in the United States.[1] More than 10,000 have secured working rights in Canada. In Australia, more than 20,000 Chinese students were accorded an opportunity to stay, although the Australian government has appeared at times to be reconsidering its offer of residency.

Many Western organizations and governments actively promoted these exchanges. Their goal, coterminous with the goals of the Chinese

---

[1] By the end of 1993, some 49,000 of the roughly 53,000 students who had applied for green cards had had their applications approved under the Chinese Student Protection Act. See Kyna Rubin, "Fifty Thousand Individual Decisions," *NAFSA Newsletter,* March 1994, p. 5.

government, was to train a new generation (or retrain an older generation) of researchers and teachers and thereby strengthen educational and
research institutes in China.[2] While many institutions have expressed
great concern for Chinese students and scholars in the wake of the 1989
Tiananmen incident, and some have provided funds to help those most
under threat to stay, these organizations recognize that if Chinese trained
abroad do not return, much of the organizations' work will have gone for
naught. Concerns also existed in the West that the Chinese government
might react to Western government policy by closing down the doors to
the outside world. While China in 1990 did initially tighten controls on
those going overseas, the overall policy has been further liberalized, and
the resultant numbers have increased.[3]

But as the political fallout of June 4 recedes, a critical question
remains whether Chinese students and scholars are planning to return to
China, and if so, in what number. What reasons motivate people to stay
or return? Do those reasons suggest that short-term changes in China,
such as the current economic boom, could lead more to return, or are
there endemic reasons that people are not returning? If economics is the
key reason that people do not return, growth in China's economy could
increase the return flow. Similarly, if Chinese in the United States are
not living very well, they may be more likely to return. On the other
hand, if politics is a critical factor, then economic growth without political liberalization may have little effect on the numbers of returnees. Is
the small number of returnees not a problem because those remaining in
the United States are transferring enough technology back to warrant a
continuation of China's "open policy"?[4] Finally, what Chinese government policies are most likely to succeed in drawing more Chinese back
to China? Are there any lessons to be learned from the experiences of
Taiwan and South Korea? How are Chinese students and scholars likely
to respond to strategies that are reported to have worked for other
developing countries? What role can international organizations and the
U.S. government play in helping to reverse the brain drain?

With these concerns in mind, the authors approached the Ford Foundation for financial support. The Ford Foundation has been one of the

---

[2] David M. Lampton, *A Relationship Restored: Trends in U.S.-China Educational Exchanges, 1978–1984* (Washington, D.C.: National Academy Press, 1986).

[3] Document No. 44 of August 1992 emphasized the right of free travel overseas, especially for those who had already been overseas; it also allowed the spouses of visiting
scholars to travel abroad to visit their spouses.

[4] For a discussion of the role of Chinese students and scholars in technology transfer,
see Leo A. Orleans, "Chinese Students and Technology Transfer," *Journal of Northeast
Asian Studies* 4.4 (Winter 1985): 1–25.

most active organizations in training Chinese, through its programs in economics, international relations, and international law. It, too, has found that few of the future teachers it has trained and funded are returning. We acknowledge their financial support, at the same time declaring that they in no way influenced our research and our findings.

This book is composed of eight chapters and five appendixes. First, borrowing from cross-national studies we highlight the major characteristics of the brain drain. We also outline the findings of recent research on the Chinese brain drain and present our own hypotheses. Second, we present a brief history of China's policy on overseas study and argue that the brain drain had already begun in 1987, although the events of June 4, 1989, exacerbated the problem, both because of the nature of those events and because of the nature of the international response to them. Chapter three sketches the backgrounds of the people in our sample and reflects on what these sketches say about the nature of the Chinese brain drain. Chapter four presents our dependent variable—an expressed view about whether or not to return to China—and then outlines the characteristics of the different groups that formed around the various responses to that question. Chapter five explains people's current choices about returning by looking at factors such as sex, family background variables, and age, as well as the effect of economics and politics. We also address certain factors that we anticipated would have an effect but, in fact, did not. In chapter six we assess the extent of the brain drain and the level of loss to China. In chapter seven we explore the question of whether the brain drain can be slowed or reversed through conscious policy measures or whether China must rely on the gradual process of economic development to solve the problem. Finally, in the conclusion we evaluate whether China's brain drain is sui generis or simply reflects another Third World country losing its best and brightest to the more developed West.

In five appendixes to the study we (1) outline our research methodology and some of the problems we confronted in trying to find a sample that reflected our goal of "randomness, reliability, and representativeness," (2) explain our use of logistic regression analysis, (3) describe and explain our structuring of the response variable, "people's views about returning," in our logistic regression analysis, (4) present President Bush's executive order of April 1990 that allowed the Chinese students and scholars to remain in the United States, and (5) present a copy of our interview protocol. Tables and figures summarizing our findings appear at the end of the book.

ONE

Explaining the Brain Drain

Cross-national studies have found a set of relatively consistent factors that both "push" people out of their homelands and "pull" them into the developed world. Most studies see the low level of economic and political development in the Third World pushing academics and other professionals out, while the resources and benefits of the developed world pull them in. Other "pull" factors include professional opportunities, living and working conditions, opportunities for employment, the presence of friends and family, and political freedom. According to Lakshmana Rao, it is the "comparison of the potential migrant's situation in his country of origin with the situation of his peers in the country of destination that is critical to the decision of the potential migrant."[1] Thus the pull of higher salaries, greater logistical support, political stability, and opportunities for mobility leads people to leave their homelands and move to the developed world.

Political factors, such as freedom, stability, and political culture, may also be important. According to El-Saati, the existence of specific criteria for evaluating performance and achievement, which decrease the importance of personal ties in affecting promotion, makes the West more attractive to people from the more traditional states who lack such connections. El-Saati also believed that Middle East intellectuals were alienated by "factors of revulsion" toward their own society when they compared it to the advanced West.[2] Political factors, such as the desire for greater civil or political rights, are also important. Based on

---

[1] Gutta Lakshmana Rao, *Brain Drain and Foreign Students: A Study of the Attitudes and Intentions of Foreign Students in Australia, the USA, Canada, and France* (Queensland, Australia: University of Queensland Press, 1979), p. 5. The same definition was used by Otieza ten years earlier. See E. Otieza, "A Differential Push-Pull Approach," in *The Brain Drain*, ed. W. Adams (New York: Macmillan, 1968), p. 126.

[2] Samia El-Saati, "Egyptian Brain Drain: Its Size, Dynamics, and Dimensions," in *Brain Drain: Proceedings from the Second Euro-Arab Social Research Group Conference*, ed. Mourad Wahba (Cairo: Ain Shams University Press, 1980), pp. 49–64.

multivariate analysis of a model testing the impact of various economic, professional, and political variables upon foreign students' decisions to remain in the United States, Huang found a significant correlation between a nation's lack of political freedom and its citizens' desire to stay in the United States. These findings prompted him to assert that "a significant proportion of non-returning students [in the United States] from some Asian and Middle Eastern countries are virtual political refugees in the sense that their stay was motivated more by the intolerability of their home country's political situation and less by professional considerations."[3]

Some studies see the roots of the brain drain in the structure of the global economy and its effect on university systems in the developing states. Many proponents of the World Systems approach argue that the colonial nature of Third World universities, and the inappropriateness of the educational training that these cultural appendages introduce, lead to the brain drain. Proponents of this theory argue that the "Third World is at the periphery of the world's educational and intellectual systems, while industrialized nations constitute the center."[4] Universities and research centers in the developed world provide the accepted theoretical models and research methods that peripheral universities, starved for resources, are forced to accept in return for financial support.[5] Scholars seeking status or recognition when they employ these methodologies gravitate to the developed world, where their skills and perspectives are valued. This factor was more true for Africa and India, where the British and other colonial powers continued to dominate the course content of universities into the 1970s, than it would be for China, where it is only since the 1980s that Chinese universities have again become integrated into the global educational system.[6]

A more purely macroeconomic explanation for the brain drain is the imbalance between the number of people trained in the developing country and the limited opportunities that exist in that country.[7] The reverse

---

[3] Wei-chiao Huang, "An Empirical Analysis of Foreign Student Brain Drain to the United States," *Economics of Education Review* 7.2 (1988): 231–43.

[4] P. G. Altbach, "Servitude of the Mind? Education, Dependency, and Neocolonialism," *Teachers College Record* 79 (December 1977): 187.

[5] Ruth Hayhoe and Jurgen Henze, "Chinese Western Scholarly Exchange and the Danger of Dependency," *Comparative Education* 20.1 (1984): 39–56.

[6] For Africa, see Ali Mazrui, "The University as a Multinational Corporation," in Ali Mazrui, *Political Values and the Educated Class in Africa* (Berkeley: University of California Press, 1978). For India, see S. K. Chopra, *Brain Drain and How to Reverse It* (New Delhi: Lancer International, 1986).

[7] J. C. Sanchez-Arnau and Elba Hermida Calvo, "International Mobility and Recognition of Studies, Diplomas, and Degrees," *Higher Education in Europe* 12.3 (1987): 62–68.

may also be true: when Western economies go into recession, thereby shrinking the available job pool within the country, foreign students are far more likely to return home, especially if expanding economies and rising standards of living in their home country increase professional opportunities at home.[8]

But while economics may play a role, "level of income is not the strongest determinant of a decision to return to the home country or to remain abroad." Individual factors are also important in the decision to emigrate. According to Glaser, social origin (or social class) and the ability to adjust to foreign social and work conditions may have a major effect on a person's decision to stay abroad.[9] Some studies also suggest that those who choose to emigrate are more self-interested than those who remain behind and have put self-interest ahead of the interests of their state.[10] According to El-Saati, people who go overseas have "an insufficient political consciousness," being more concerned about their own research than about the national good.[11] In the Chinese context, this would mean placing less importance on collectivist and "state-socialist" values and more importance on individual advancement.

Taiwan's experience can help us discern why Chinese might choose not to go home and the conditions under which they might begin to return in larger numbers. From a comparative perspective, Taiwan shares cultural and social similarities with China and also experienced a very severe brain drain. From 1950 to 1980, an estimated 80,000 university graduates left Taiwan to study abroad.[12] During the 1960s, only five of every hundred university graduates who went abroad for advanced studies returned to live in Taiwan. In 1967 alone, 2,109 professional, technical, and similarly qualified Taiwanese migrated to the United States.[13] Moreover, once these students left, they left for good. An estimated 86 percent of Taiwanese science students in the United States

---

[8] Huang, "Empirical Analysis," 238.

[9] William Glaser, *The Brain Drain: Emigration and Return* (New York: Pergamon Press, 1978).

[10] Although China's government may not formally espouse this view, it does reflect the views of the more conservative forces in the State Education Commission and other conservative institutions, who see those who return late as less than pure, not only because of the ideological influence of their time abroad, but also because they did not respond to their unit's request to return on time.

[11] El-Saati, "Egyptian Brain Drain," p. 61.

[12] R. King, "Taiwan Launches New Program," *Chronicle of Higher Education* 26 (October 1988): 27.

[13] Heather Low Ruth, "Taiwan," in *The International Migration of High-Level Manpower: Its Impact on the Development Process,* ed. Committee on the International Migration of Talent (New York: Praeger, 1970).

changed their visa status from student to immigrant in 1967, compared to 46 percent from the rest of the developing world.

Taiwanese were pulled to the United States by the same factors affecting other migrants cited above. In a 1971 survey, scholars rated the following as strong factors pulling them to stay in the United States: better facilities, higher salaries, a more intellectual atmosphere, more political freedom, and more academic freedom.[14] By the 1980s, these factors had not changed much. Chang lists several of the same pull factors and lists low salaries, a lack of political and economic freedom, and a poor intellectual atmosphere as factors pushing people to the United States.[15] Because of cultural similarities, one could assume that many of the factors affecting Taiwan's brain drain of the 1960s may be active elements in the decisions of mainland scholars in the 1980s not to return.

Factors leading people to leave in the first place may differ from those factors that convince them to stay abroad. Song argues that although economic factors were most important in the early stages of South Korean outmigration, the strength of the Korean economy was not enough to pull people back as Korea developed.[16] Instead, psychological and emotional factors became the most prominent reasons why people chose to stay in the United States. The following data show this fact to be true. Korean scientists were asked at two different times to choose the three most important factors for remaining in the United States. While still students in their degree programs they listed "more training and educational experiences" (65 percent), "United States is the best place for accomplishment" (45 percent), and "have a good job in America" (34 percent). When the same people were asked the same question after finishing their degree, they chose "family situation makes it difficult to return" (55 percent), "have a good job in America" (47 percent), and "the United States is the best place for accomplishments" (37 percent). The change over these two time periods can be attributed at least in part to the fact that people had already received their training and now had children who had grown up in the United States who might not be able to readjust to Korean society.

---

[14] C. H. C. Kao, *Brain Drain: A Case Study of China* (Taipei: Mei Ya Publications, 1971).

[15] Shirley Chang, "Causes of Brain Drain and Solutions: The Taiwan Experience," *Studies in Comparative International Development* 27.1 (Spring 1992): 32.

[16] Ha-Joong Song, "Who Stays? Who Returns? The Choices of Korean Scientists and Engineers" (Ph.D. dissertation, Kennedy School of Government, Harvard University, 1991).

Findings of the Literature on the Chinese Brain Drain

The first major study about Chinese students in the United States, by Leo Orleans, focused mostly on establishing how many Chinese students and scholars, holding what types of visas, were in the United States.[17] Orleans also described in detail the problems faced by returnees and showed that the numbers of returnees had decreased because of the 1987 "anti–bourgeois liberalization" campaign. In subsequent studies and reports, Orleans has raised several important questions, such as whether or not there really has been a brain "loss." Arguing that China had a finite need for scientists and researchers and that only a small number would be able to find jobs at prestigious coastal institutions, Orleans asserted that China was overproducing advanced researchers. Therefore, if a large number decided to stay in the West, it was no great loss to China.

Since the Tiananmen incident and the Western decision to offer asylum to tens of thousands of Chinese students and scholars, other studies on the Chinese brain drain have emerged. One of the best studies, by Chang and Deng, applied the push/pull concept and used a survey of 568 students at ten universities to flesh out the usual economic and political factors.[18] In their 1989 survey, politics loomed large: in response to the Tiananmen events, 72.6 percent of respondents stated that they were most concerned about the political situation. Yet problems of career and readjustment to life in China were also strong motivators for not returning, as 71.3 percent were concerned about their ability to readjust to China and 61.3 percent were not optimistic about their future career prospects. Five other factors influenced this outmigration: pressure from family and friends to stay abroad, foreign values and growing individualism among the Chinese students in the United States, limited financial incentives from Chinese units to return and their need to help home-grown Ph.D.s first, ineffective Chinese government efforts to force students to return, and cold relations between China and foreign governments, which prevented China from pressuring foreign states to stop the brain drain.

---

17 See Leo A. Orleans, *Chinese Students in America: Policies, Issues, and Numbers* (Washington, D.C.: National Academy Press, 1988).

18 Parris Chang and Zhiduan Deng, "The Chinese Brain Drain and Policy Options," *Studies in Comparative International Development* 27.1 (Spring 1992): 44–60. For their study they sent out 1,782 surveys; of the 1,746 surveys received by students, 568 were returned, for a response rate of 32.5 percent. Response rates at this level are troubling. Sociologists prefer response rates of 50 percent or better because otherwise some inherent bias may have affected who does and who does not respond.

Other studies have reinforced some of these findings. For example, according to Ren, the United States remains a popular symbol in China, and family and friends in China pressure students to stay abroad and serve as a bridge for others to traverse.[19] Similarly, Zhang found that political concerns were the most important reasons people did not return.[20] Nevertheless, the notion that staying overseas changed people's attitudes was challenged in part by Zhao and Xie, who found that age of the foreign student and the amount of time he or she spent reading the *New York Times,* and not the length of time he or she had lived in the United States, was the best predictor of attitudes toward the government.[21] Older scholars were more responsive to government propaganda and its political viewpoints than younger scholars and students. Therefore, as our study shows, older people are more likely to return.

Political attitudes have had some effect on views about returning. Soon after Tiananmen, Gu found very strong antigovernment political attitudes among students and scholars he surveyed and similarly strong attitudes against returning. According to Gu's survey, over 82 percent of Chinese students and scholars preferred the Northern European (28.8 percent) or the American (54.0 percent) system of government, with only 0.5 percent preferring the PRC system and only 0.9 percent preferring the Taiwanese system.[22] But these political values had changed because of Tiananmen. Although 34 percent said they would have voted for the Chinese Communist Party before the Tiananmen events, those events brought the percentage down to only 6.9 percent. Similarly, Zhang found that while only 6.1 percent had planned to seek permanent residence status in the United States before Tiananmen, 31.0 percent

---

[19] Ren Donglai, "The Popular Images of the United States in China Today" (paper presented at the China Forum, Center for Chinese Studies, University of California, Berkeley, April 1, 1993).

[20] See Xiaoping Zhang, "Residential Preferences: A Brain Drain Study on Chinese Students in the United States" (Ph.D. dissertation, Graduate School of Education, Harvard University, 1992). This study set out to prove that politics, not economics, was the dominant factor, and questions were presented in a manner that was likely to confirm, rather than challenge, that hypothesis. Still, most studies carried out immediately after Tiananmen found similar results.

[21] Xinshu Zhao and Yu Xie, "Western Influence on (People's Republic of China) Chinese Students in the United States," *Comparative Education Review* 36.4 (November 1992). Weiqun Gu also found no correlation between student's year of arrival in the United States and professed political philosophy. See Weiqun Gu, "Chinese Students and Scholars in American Universities and Their Political Attitudes" (unpublished paper). Yet when Chang and Deng asked students, 46.2 percent said that their political views had changed greatly since coming to the United States. Chang and Deng, "Chinese Brain Drain," p. 46.

[22] Gu, "Political Attitudes."

planned to do so after Tiananmen.[23] Also, while the majority (57.9 percent) had said that before Tiananmen they were definitely planning to return upon graduation, after the event the majority said that they planned to wait to see how the political situation in China developed. No doubt Tiananmen did play a strong role in convincing Chinese students and scholars that China was politically unstable, and therefore many studies done soon after June 4, 1989, showed very strong concerns on these issues, which were often presented as the key reason for people's choosing not to return.

Nevertheless, economic factors were still at work even in the wake of Tiananmen. At least one study showed that salary or income differentials, a better professional and academic environment (including better facilities and access to international conferences), and personal factors, such as ability to adjust to different cultures, strength of family ties, marital status, and concerns about children's education, affected the decision to return.[24]

One nonquantitative study by Brzezinski, which employed in-depth interviews, tapped deeply into the goals and desires of six Chinese male students in the United States.[25] The main contribution of this study was to stress the importance of personal values, such as the search for prestige, honor, respect, fairness and, though not directly addressed by the study, the importance of self-realization, as key factors motivating young Chinese to go to university, go overseas to study, and then seriously to contemplate not returning to China. In his open-ended interviews, Brzezinski also found that the students never referred to politics as a reason to stay, though they did speak at length about the problems of the work unit system, which they said bred jealousy rather than healthy competition.

In the end, most studies, such as that by Kao and Liu, found that a mix of motives pushed people out of China and kept them abroad. These factors include a poor work environment, low income, poor housing, limited job mobility and promotional opportunities, political instability, and the political capriciousness of the system, as well as the lack of academic freedom.[26]

---

[23] Zhang, "Residential Preferences," p. 64.

[24] Huisong Yuan, "Brain Drain from the Third World Countries to the West: A Case Study of Chinese Graduate Students Currently Studying in Canadian Universities" (paper prepared for the Canadian International Development Agency, November 1991), p. 34.

[25] See Michael Brzezinski, *Migration and Opportunity: A Qualitative Understanding of the Chinese Student Brain Drain Phenomenon,* NAFSA Working Paper, no. 41 (Washington, D.C.: NAFSA, 1994).

[26] Che-han Kao and Ch'i-hua Liu, "On the Chinese Communist Party's Policies to Encourage the Return of Scholars Studying Abroad," *Zhongguo dalu yanjiu* (Research on

Our Hypotheses about China's Brain Drain

Based upon these studies and our own assumptions, we developed some hypotheses, which we tested in our study. First, we hypothesized that by 1993 the initial political reaction to Tiananmen had run its course and that economic factors, particularly better living conditions and work facilities, were now likely to be the most important factors. We sought to challenge the arguments of many American politicians, Taiwanese scholars, and mainland dissidents that Chinese wanted to stay in the United States because of their fears of political persecution. Also, given the tight controls that a Chinese work unit (*danwei*) has over its employees,[27] we believed that the "political culture" of the Chinese work environment, including the power of one's supervisor and problems with co-workers, as well as the overall severe limitations on job mobility, would influence people's decisions.

Second, we expected that family factors would be an important influence. Having taught Chinese students in the United States, Zweig was always struck by the way attitudes about returning changed sharply when a student's spouse joined him (or her) in the United States. We hypothesized that these views would be strengthened by the arrival of children.

Third, we wanted to collect more systematic information about the quality of life of the Chinese students and scholars in the United States. If economic conditions were important in affecting the decision to return, we needed to know if the Chinese were "making it" in the United States and if they were more likely to return if they were not enjoying material success.

Finally, we wondered about the real costs of the brain drain. If Chinese overseas were making major contributions to their units and families back home, or if they were promoting Sino-American business exchanges, it would be good for the mainland. In 1987, during a major debate over the lack of returnees, Zhao Ziyang, then the party's general secretary, argued that the brain drain was in reality a case of "storing brainpower overseas" that would be useful in the future.[28] For his argument to be true, Chinese overseas need to have strong ties back home

---

mainland China), 35.6 (June 1992): 41–45 (in Chinese).

[27] See Andrew Walder, *Communist Neo-Traditionalism* (Berkeley: University of California Press, 1986); and Michael Cohen and Gail Henderson, *The Chinese Hospital* (New Haven, Conn.: Yale University Press, 1984).

[28] This 1987 quote is attributed to former party general secretary Zhao Ziyang, who justified continued educational openness even as the number of returnees declined. Xu Lin, lecture at Fairbank Center for East Asian Research, Boston, Mass., August 14, 1990.

and should be helping China in some way. With these issues in mind, we composed our questionnaire and built our sample (see appendixes A and D).

TWO

The Shifting Policy on Overseas Study and Its Effect on the Brain Drain

After the hiatus of the Cultural Revolution, educational exchanges with the West began again in 1972–73, with England, Australia, France, Italy, New Zealand, Canada, and other countries that had established diplomatic relations and cultural exchanges. During this time, the numbers were extremely small, and there were few if any "defections."[1] The pace of exchanges increased dramatically in the late 1970s, particularly after the 1978 Sino-American Understanding on Educational Exchanges (October 1978) and the 1979 Agreement on Cooperation in Science and Technology (January 1979). Until the mid-1980s, most educational exchanges were controlled by the Ministry of Education (later renamed the State Education Commission; hereafter SEDC), and the vast majority of sojourners who went abroad as visiting scholars were key researchers in many of China's top research institutes. These "key elements" (*gu gan*) returned on time, usually after one or two years, and took up major positions in their home institutions. Based on interviews in China, Chen and Zweig found that many of them had never even considered staying abroad.[2]

Beginning in 1982, as part of China's Sixth Five-Year Plan (1981–85), the number of people going abroad increased as international organizations and foreign governments commenced long-term development

---

[1] From 1972 to 1976, altogether 1,629 students were sent to 49 countries. See Huang Shiqi, "Contemporary Educational Relations with the Industrialized World," in *China's Education and the Industrialized World: Studies in Cultural Transfer,* ed. Ruth Hayhoe and Marianne Bastid (Armonk, N.Y.: M. E. Sharpe, 1987), pp. 225–51. In those days, if students or scholars (who were almost uniformly sent by the government) had not returned, it would have been called a "defection." In that light, one can only be amazed at the transition that occurred in Chinese government attitudes toward the brain drain in the 1980s.

[2] Chen Changgui and David Zweig, "The Impact of the Open Policy on Higher Education in China" (paper presented at the Association for Asian Studies annual meeting, Los Angeles, March 25–28, 1993).

assistance to Chinese research and academic institutions. China joined the World Bank in 1979–80 and soon after sent students abroad as part of its first, fourth, and ninth World Bank loans.[3] Organizations such as the Canadian International Development Agency (1982), the United Nations Development Program (1983), and the Ford Foundation (1983) offered assistance to the Ministry of Education, which dispersed these opportunities to universities throughout China. Many of the recipients of these awards went overseas for Ph.D.s and were still abroad in 1989 at the time of the Tiananmen incident.

In 1984–85, the system of allocating spots overseas underwent a major change as the decentralization of exchanges to the individual universities allowed for a greater number of linkage opportunities.[4] Universities and their departments were empowered to make their own educational links and exchanges, provided they used their own funds, and the role of SEDC-organized exchanges decreased, particularly for the "key" (*zhong dian*) schools, which were well connected with foreign schools and therefore able to facilitate many of these exchanges on their own. Also, in December 1984, China introduced a more liberal policy on "people who study abroad at their own expense," making it easier for those people who could make their own arrangements to go abroad, sparking a "fever to study abroad."[5] Thus large numbers went overseas in 1985–86. For example, the number of formal exchange scholars from Huazhong University of Science and Technology in Wuhan, a key SEDC school, peaked in 1985 at 140. While many of them were called "self-supporting," the majority, who kept their jobs at home, were called "self-paying, publicly sent" (*zi fei, danwei gong pai*), which was the state's preferred arrangement. This way, the SEDC hoped that educational units in China could maintain links with the scholars after they went abroad, even if the schools were not paying for their studies abroad.[6]

---

3 Ruth Hayhoe, *China's Universities and the Open Door* (Armonk, N.Y.: M. E. Sharpe, 1989).

4 "Decision of the CCP-CC on Reform of the Educational System, 27 May 1985," in Foreign Broadcast Information Service, *Daily Report—China* (FBIS-CHI), 30 May 1985, pp. K1–K11. For analyses of the May decision see Stanley Rosen, "Recentralization, Decentralization, and Rationalization: Deng Xiaoping's Bifurcated Educational Policy," *Modern China* 11.3 (July 1985): 301–46; Ruth Hayhoe, "China's Higher Curricular Reform in Historical Perspective," *China Quarterly*, June 1987, pp. 196–230; and Keith Lewin, "Science Education in China: Transformation and Changes in the 1980s," *Comparative Education Review* 31 (August 1987): 419–41.

5 See Xiao Hang, "Do Not Disregard Study Abroad Fever," *Gaojian zhanxian*, no. 3 (13 March 1986): 39, in FBIS-CHI, 10 July 1986, pp. 18–19.

6 "Provisional Regulations on People Who Study Abroad at Their Own Expense, 26 December 1984," *Zhongguo jiaoyu bao* (China education news), 26 January 1985, in *Chinese*

Real concerns about people not returning emerged in early 1987.[7] After nationwide student protests in December 1986, Deng Xiaoping cracked down, removed party leader Hu Yaobang from office, and began a brief "anti–bourgeois liberalization" campaign. Students in the United States expressed their concerns to the Communist Party in a series of letters. Following this incident, the number of Chinese students in the United States applying for visa extensions increased significantly. The number of people applying for extensions in 1987 increased by 22 percent over 1986, the largest percentage increase of any year between 1983 and 1991.[8] Adding to these students' concerns was the case of Yang Wei, a Chinese student who had completed his graduate studies at the University of Arizona.[9] After returning to China, he was arrested, tried, and convicted for articles criticizing Chinese government policies that he had written while he was in the United States. Also in 1987, the Chinese government tightened its policy on going abroad.[10] Still, the main reason for the decline in returnees was that very few people really wanted to go back; many had already begun to look for chances to stay longer or extend their study time; others quit their studies and went to work. Many who had finished their theses went to work while their spouses went to school. A main purpose was to maintain their student status and stay in the United States as long as possible.

In response to this drop in the number of returnees, the Chinese government called on the U.S. government for help. During his June 1987 trip to the United States, He Dongchang, deputy minister of the SEDC, called on the United States to do more to "encourage" Chinese students to return home and to tighten loopholes in U.S. visa laws that the Chinese government claimed were facilitating the overextension of visas. The Chinese strategy involved making all junior faculty at Chinese colleges apply for J-1 student visas, rather than the F-1 student visas they had been receiving.[11] Under J-1 student visas, Chinese students could not shift to a work visa without first going home for two

---

Education 31.1 (Spring 1988): 25–28.

7 See "Vice-Premier Li Peng Speaks on Improving the Work of Sending Students Abroad," *Liaowang,* 22 December 1986, pp. 3–4, in Joint Publications Research Service (JPRS)-CPS-87-011, 13 March 1987.

8 Calculations were based on the numbers presented in a table in Liu Shengji, "Research and Analysis concerning Non-returning Mainland Scholars Who Came to the United States," *Zhongguo dalu yanjiu* 33.8 (1991): 59 (in Chinese).

9 *China Daily,* 22 December 1987, p. 3.

10 See "Certain Interim Provisions of the State Education Commission on the Work of Sending Personnel Abroad," in JPRS-CAR-87-024, 23 July 1987, p. 89. The document had been drafted in late 1986.

11 *China Exchange News* 15.3 (September 1987): 17; 15.4 (December 1987): 17.

years. (These same rules had always applied to visiting scholars, who also came on J-1 visas.) However, because of the Tiananmen incident the following year and subsequent U.S. policy, this strategy did not increase the number of returnees.

But because so many Chinese students and scholars were in the United States, having extended their stays since the mid-1980s, the effect of June 4, 1989, and the U.S. government decision to let people stay was immense. If not for the Tiananmen incident, many more of the Ph.D.s who had been funded by international agencies might have returned once their options to stay wore out. Although many had not wanted to go back, they thought they might have to. Thus when asked if before Tiananmen they had expected to return to China, most students and scholars replied in the affirmative. But once the U.S. and Canadian governments responded to the events of June 4 by making it easy for them to stay, the number who decided not to go back immediately or soon increased dramatically.[12]

The Chinese government introduced far more restrictive measures on overseas studies in 1989, stipulating that any university graduate who applied for overseas studies had to work for a minimum of three to five years in a public organization or pay up to 10,000 RMB for each year short of five.[13] But this policy change, while initially horrifying to most Chinese, did not retard the flow. First, immediately after June 4, the number of applicants to the United States increased, as did the number of visas given out by the U.S. government. Second, many Chinese have been able to borrow the funds to pay off the government or their unit to buy their way out. Third, this policy favored people with "overseas ties," as they were most likely to be able to buy their way out of China.

The historical context of our survey in terms of the history of educational exchange is also important. While much of the research on China's brain drain cited above was done in the wake of Tiananmen, and therefore may have its own historical bias, our study was influenced by two major events. First, in January 1992 Deng Xiaoping made his famous "trip to the south" (*nan xun*), which triggered a much more liberal economic and cultural climate in China. Significant economic

---

[12] When asked if June 4 was important to their decision about whether or not to return, 38.9 percent of our respondents said that it was very important or somewhat important. But whether it was important because they could get a green card or because it made them feel that China was insecure is unclear. Also, that only 38.9 percent felt it important or somewhat important suggests that its importance has declined in the past four years.

[13] "Supplemental Regulations of Self-funded Study Abroad for Applicants at University Level and Higher, 10 February 1990." For a good discussion of this document, see *Kuang chiao ching* (Wide angle), 16 April 1990, in JPRS-CAR-90-049, 11 July 1990, pp. 7–10.

growth, in the light of a continued economic slump in the West, increased the interest among Chinese to return to China to do business, especially among people who had good political or economic connections. Also, Deng's trip affected China's policies on overseas studies. In August 1992, China introduced a more liberal policy which, on paper, allowed students and scholars to come and go freely (*lai qu ziyou*). It also included new incentives aimed at bringing people home.[14] Returnees were now allowed to go to any unit of their choice, in any city of their choice, rather than having to return to their home unit. The result has been an increase of returnees to places such as Shenzhen and an increase in the number of visits by Chinese students. Many scholars have shown a preference for going to Hong Kong, where they can find Chinese culture in a more open political and economic environment and salaries that rival those in the West.

The second event was the looming opportunity for many of our respondents to apply for permanent residence status in the United States under the 1992 "Chinese Student Protection Act." According to that law, any Chinese who had been in the United States before April 1990 and who had not returned to China for more than sixty days was eligible to apply for a green card. As many as 60,000 Chinese were expected to apply for green cards between July 1, 1993, and June 30, 1994. In the end, 53,000 people applied and 49,000 applications were approved.[15] As a result, many people we approached in spring 1993 were concerned about whether talking with us might complicate their applications. The Chinese attitude that "doing less leads to fewer problems" (*xiao zuo, xiao cuo*) was at work. As a result, numerous Chinese chose the low-risk strategy of not meeting with us.

---

[14] "Returning Students Find Jobs at Home," *China Daily*, 22 May 1993.
[15] Rubin, "Fifty Thousand Individual Decisions," pp. 5, 38–40.

THREE

Characteristics and Profiles of the Sample

While we have described many of the specific details of our survey procedures in appendix A, it is important to outline briefly several key aspects of our research strategy. First, because we wanted to be able to generalize from our example, we chose a stratified random sample based on various locations, different fields, and differing statuses in the United States (i.e., visiting scholars, current students, and people out of school and in the workforce). For each locality where we carried out interviews, we compiled a list of names of students in several schools and then chose randomly from each list. We did the same for those in the workforce, asking Chinese friends to give us lists of names of their friends. As we explain in appendix A, we were unable to do this for visiting scholars. The numbers were too small and changed yearly; instead, we simply ensured representation from both sexes and from different fields, age groups, and different lengths of time in the United States. Second, rather than using a mailed questionnaire, we employed face-to-face interviews based on a 105-question questionnaire, which we pretested in Toronto and then revised for use in the United States. While we hoped that using face-to-face interviews would increase our yield—a rejection rate of above 50 percent, which can happen with a mailed survey, would call the representativeness of our sample into question—we still experienced a refusal rate averaging 25–30 percent. Nevertheless, our findings, the frankness of the responses, and the variety of people we interviewed make us confident that we tapped views that represent those of a cross section of Chinese students, scholars, and former students in America.

Still, the issue of reliability of responses remains problematic. We believe that some people, for reasons of "face," said they "might" return when they really did not plan to do so. Thus we put people who said they "probably would return but did not know when" into the broad group of non-returnees. Also, because Chinese are brought up to put issues of morality above personal material interests, people may have chosen politics, rather than economics, as the reason for staying, again for reasons of face. Nevertheless, so many people chose economic factors as their primary justification for not returning that, although the effect of this variable may be understated, it is a statistically significant factor predicting views about returning in our overall model. So again we feel that we have been able to tap into most people's real motivations. Also, the admission by almost 50 percent of our sample that they never had planned to return to China strengthens our conviction that most people spoke frankly and truthfully. The following list gives a brief introduction to our population sample.

1. Dates of arrival for sample: see figure 1
2. Total number of people interviewed: 273
3. Number of people interviewed in each locality:
   Albuquerque: 52 (19 percent)
   Boston: 79 (28.9 percent)
   Buffalo: 45 (16.5 percent)
   California: 72 (26.4 percent)[1]
   New York City: 25 (9.2 percent)
4. Classification of interviewees (by current visa type):
   F-1 (student): 147 (53.8 percent)[2]
   J-1 (exchange or visiting scholar): 36 (13.2 percent)
   J-1 (student): 22 (8.1 percent)
   H (temporary worker): 18 (6.6 percent)
   B (tourist, visitor): 4 (1.5 percent)
   G-4 (international employee): 1 (0.4 percent)
   Permanent resident of United States: 28 (10.3 percent)
   American citizen: 7 (2.6 percent)
   Missing data: 10 (3.6 percent)
5. Sex:[3]
   Males: 192 (70.3 percent)
   Females: 80 (29.3 percent)
   Missing data: 1
6. Marital status (of 264 cases):[4]
   Married: 195 (73.9 percent)

---

[1] Most of our interviews in California were in Los Angeles or San Diego, with additional interviews in the greater Bay Area.

[2] The large number of F-1 visas results from the fact that under the president's executive order of April 1990, J-1 students and scholars were allowed to change to F-1 visa status.

[3] The number of women in our sample approximated the overall percentage of women, as compared to men, who received visas to study in the United States (see p. 36).

[4] In her 1989–90 study, Zhang Xiaoping found a much smaller percentage of married people. We cannot explain the different findings.

Single: 59 (22.3 percent)
Divorced: 10 (3.8 percent)
Missing data: 9 (3.4 percent)
7. Parental background characteristics (for 270 respondents):[5]
High-ranking cadres: 16 (5.9 percent)
Middle-ranking cadres: 50 (18.5 percent)
Workers: 26 (9.6 percent)
Peasants: 21 (7.8 percent)
Intellectuals (job in a university): 141 (52.2 percent)
Business background: 5 (1.9 percent)
Other: 11 (4.1 percent)
Missing data: 3 (1.1 percent)
8. Level of education before leaving China:
Undergraduate education: 132 (48.4 percent)
Master's degree: 120 (44 percent)
Ph.D. degree: 9 (3.3 percent)
Other: 11 (4 percent)
Missing data: 1
9. Top five cities of origin in China (for 218 respondents):
Beijing: 95 (43.6 percent)[6]
Shanghai: 39 (17.9 percent)
Nanjing: 13 (6.0 percent)
Wuhan: 12 (5.5 percent)
Guangzhou: 7 (3.2 percent)
Other, coastal: 23 (10.6 percent)
Other, noncoastal: 29 (13.3 percent)
Missing data: 55
10. Residence of interviewees' spouses:[7]
With them in the United States: 162 (59.3 percent)
Still in China: 39 (14.3 percent)
No response (unmarried): 71 (26 percent)
No data: 1
11. Number of people with children: 136 (49.8 percent)

---

[5] Because these findings are remarkably similar to the numbers Gu found in his survey, we believe that we were tapping into a somewhat representative sample of the general population. We realize, of course, that according to the rules of probability sampling, we cannot really claim that our sample is scientifically representative of the entire population of Chinese students in the United States.

[6] Percentages are only for those for whom we have data.

[7] Although only 195 people are currently married, 201 reported the residence of their spouses (i.e., 6 of the 10 people who were divorced responded to our question about spouse's place of residence).

12. Residence of interviewees' children:
    With them in the United States: 85 (31.5 percent)
    Not in United States: 51 (18.7 percent)
    No response (unmarried/childless/no data): 136 (49.8 percent)
13. Specialization:
    Natural sciences: 64 (23.4 percent)
    Applied sciences (incl. engineering, medicine): 92 (33.7 percent)
    Business or management: 16 (5.9 percent)
    Applied social sciences (law, economics): 23 (8.4 percent)
    Social sciences: 30 (11.0 percent)
    Humanities and fine arts (incl. education, history): 32 (11.7 percent)
    Other: 2 (0.7 percent)
    No response: 14 (5.1 percent)
14. Annual household income levels: see figure 2
15. Quality of housing: see figure 3
16. Social interaction:
    Almost exclusively with other Chinese: 18 (6.6 percent)
    Mostly with other Chinese: 152 (55.7 percent)
    About equally with Chinese and non-Chinese: 90 (33.0 percent)
    Mostly with non-Chinese: 8 (2.9 percent)
    Missing data: 5 (1.8 percent)

Profiles of Our Sample: Views on Returning

In this section, we present profiles of the people we interviewed based on what their views were about returning. Drawing on our conversations with our interviewees, we try to determine what type of people fall into the different categories. What type of people are most likely to return? What kinds of experiences have led people to declare that they will never return? How do the people in the different categories feel about China? Therefore, before we look at explanations for people's views about returning, we need to clarify our dependent or outcome variable (question 77), describe our sample's views about returning, and present profiles of the people who fell into the seven categories. Of the 273 people we interviewed, we have data from 267 people about their views of returning. The breakdown of attitudes is presented in table 1 and figure 4.

The response to question 77 does not indicate a true decision about returning except for people in the two extreme categories. Only those people appear fully committed to a course of action. Others' answer to this question reflects both their own views about returning and their

evaluation of the possibilities of staying. We say this because if we simply had asked people if they planned to return, many would have said
yes, but such a response might not tell us very much about the likelihood
of their returning. In reality, except for the people in category 1, few
people really want to return any time soon. But if they came after April
1990, their answers about returning reflected their recognition that they
may not be able to stay in the United States after they complete their
program. Thus, if they thought it would be difficult for them to make
arrangements to stay, they leaned toward saying they would go back.
Therefore, we took our respondents' answers as only one factor on which
to determine whether or not they might return. Thus within the group
that was leaning toward returning, we put those who were only "probably" returning and those who were "definitely" returning in different
categories; among those who were "definitely returning," we differentiated between those who had already made concrete plans to return and
those who had not; and among those "probably" returning, we
differentiated between those who had kept up strong ties with China and
those who had not.

Group 1: Definitely returning and have made plans to go home

Of the 8.1 percent who are "definitely returning and have made plans
to do so," the majority are short-term visiting scholars (72.7 percent),
who came for a fixed period and have a fixed income from a fixed
source. When their time is up, their funds will be cut off. Unless they
find some new opportunity, they will go home. Because we did most of
our interviews from February to May, these visiting scholars already
knew that they had little or no opportunity to stay, so they picked
category 1. Had we interviewed them soon after they arrived in the
United States, such as in September or October when they might still
have hoped to find another opportunity, they might have picked category
2. These people also tend to have poorer English language skills, and
our findings show that there is a linear relationship between people's
views about going home and their English language skills. Most important is that these people in category 1 who have plans to go home have
significantly poorer English language skills than everyone else.[8]

We added the idea that they had to have made arrangements because
in our pretest in Toronto, many people said they would "definitely"
return, but few had made any specific plans.[9] As long as they had not

---

[8] While the mean score on returning for all people who reported their English language
level was 2.05, the mean score for people in category 1 who were returning was 2.50.

[9] Because visiting scholars comprised 25 percent of our sample population in the Toron-

made specific plans, there was still a good probability that if they found a new research or employment opportunity, they might extend their stay indefinitely. Therefore, in our U.S. interviews, we differentiated between those who "definitely planned to go back but had no plans" and people in category 1, who are basically on their way back.

One striking fact is how few of the people we interviewed planned to return immediately to live in China. Perhaps because we interviewed many graduate students who were still pursuing their degrees, the number of people with immediate plans to return was quite small. On the other hand, in the immediate aftermath of Tiananmen, often less than 3 percent of students who responded to surveys said that they were definitely going back. Still, our strong sense from the interviews was that if given the choice, very few people would return permanently any time soon.

Other than visiting scholars, who else might be returning? The economic boom in China and the opportunities for people with good personal "connections" (*guanxi*) to make large sums of money is leading people from well-placed families to consider returning. For example, one couple we know, who were not part of our sample, are the son and daughter-in-law of a former high-ranking diplomat. In the summer of 1994 they returned to China to work in the foreign sector. This view has also been reflected in the Chinese press in the United States. *Democratic China*, for instance, told of a twenty-seven-year-old woman who had gone to Canada on a World Bank loan. She was currently working in an import-export company, and although she could have applied for a Canadian residence permit, she told the magazine interviewer that she was definitely returning. Why? Originally she had thought of staying because there are so many good things in Canada; but now she believed that she could make lots of money in China, as many of her and her husband's friends were doing. Also, she felt that in China it was easy to use public money as if it were one's personal wealth. If she stayed in Canada, she would have to work very hard to make a good income, but as she had a child to care for, she wanted to make money without working too hard.[10] Because of her excellent connections, she felt that she could do this in China.

---

to interview group, the percentage of people who said they were returning was too high and not representative of the real population at all. Visiting scholars comprised 13.2 percent of our current survey, a figure that probably still overrepresents their true numbers.

[10] See "Liu si jie yu hui guo ri" (The anniversary of June 4 and the "fever to return home"), *Minzhu Zhongguo* (Democratic China), 7.16 (1993): 47.

Group 2: Definitely will return but don't know when

The 24.1 percent who "definitely will return but don't know when" feel good about China, are not alienated from the current regime, had good relations with their work unit supervisor, and are not too worried that if they go back they will have major problems. They strongly believe that they will go back; perhaps in their minds they are 70 percent likely to return. The main difference between them and the people in category 1 is that those in category 2 have not decided when to return.

Subgroups within this group, however, hold two different views about returning. One subgroup thought they would return within two to three years after graduation.[11] They want to work in the United States for a few years to build a nest egg. This plan is especially attractive to those people who came after April 1990 because they face the probability of having to go back eventually. By staying a few years after graduation, they could return to China with a foreign degree and some foreign savings.

A second subgroup may not return for ten years or more—after they have retired, perhaps, or after their children have completed school. But they feel close to China, so they really do plan to return at some point.

Group 3: Probably going back and have kept close ties to China

The 19.4 percent who are "probably going back and have kept close ties to China" have less commitment to return to China than people in category 2, but they may have stronger links with people in China than those in category 2.[12] Because they were satisfied with their jobs, have good ties with their home units, and believe they have excellent opportunities for promotion back in China, they maintain strong ties back home. Thus, some may return in the future. Nevertheless, their likelihood of returning varies according to how they understood the idea "have kept close links with China." Those links can take four forms: (1) links with their original unit (often through helping the unit with information, trips to the United States, giving or arranging lectures back home, or helping people arrange trips abroad); (2) links with colleagues

---

[11] These people reflect the same views as Gu Weiqun's "mid-term" group, who planned to return in the medium term.

[12] We cross-checked this response with their response to a question about links with China and found that their mean score on "links with home unit" is higher than that of those in every other category except those in category 1 (who are on their way back and therefore by necessity have kept up close links). This type of internal consistency among responses in our survey increases our confidence that people were relatively forthright with us.

in their original unit, but not necessarily with the unit's leaders; (3) links with family and friends, not just colleagues; and (4) links with other units in China, whether educational or business relations. People in the first two categories do not want to cut off their ties to their original unit, nor do they have problems with their unit. If things do not go well in the United States, they can easily return to China. On the other hand, people who have links only with their family or with other units, while likely to return for short visits or to make regular trips home, have few professional reasons for returning, and therefore are not likely to return to live. Their views on returning are more dependent on how things change in China and in the United States than are those of people in category 2.

Group 4: Can't really say now

Chinese who go overseas have a complex relationship with China and with their host country. They often have a "love-hate" relationship with China, based on warm memories of family and friends, and even love of their country. But they also have hostile memories of the political tumult and the suffering their families endured during various political campaigns. They have hopes for China's future, and if China were to do well, they might want to share in that future. But they also have hopes for themselves and their families in the United States and possess many quashed hopes for China as well. Emotionally, they cannot completely settle in the United States, but neither can they resettle back home.

Most of these people who "can't really say now" do not want to return, but because they have not found a good job yet, or because they came after April 1990 (half the people in this category came after April 1990), they say they have not decided (19.4 percent). If these people find a good opportunity in the United States, they will stay for a long time. Still, they have not made a public decision about not going back. Perhaps for reasons of face they do not want to say they are not going back. So they cannot make a decision.[13]

Group 5: Probably will go back but have not kept up ties

The 9.5 percent who "probably will go back but have not kept up ties" listed "face" as a primary reason for returning. Therefore, they belong best in the non-return category. Although they may return, they

---

[13] Initially, we placed this group at the end, but after doing some of our analysis it seemed far more appropriate to place them in the middle of our scale on views about returning.

are more likely not to. They also may have interpreted this category as including those who planned to go back for a short visit. And although we explained to them that returning meant "to live" (*ding zhu*), some who knew that they were not going to live in China again may have interpreted the question in a way that would allow them to say that they still may go back.

Many of these people came before 1990 (61.5 percent), but have few links with China. They are not very cognizant of what is going on in China and talk mostly about the China they knew, rather than today's China. When evaluating their current situation in the United States, they compare today's United States to the China they left, not to the current China.

Group 6: Not very likely to go back, but might if things changed in China greatly

Most of the 9.9 percent who answered that they are "not very likely to go back, but might if things changed in China greatly" will never return short of the collapse of Communist Party rule or China's switching to a purely capitalist system. Some of these people had political problems related to the Tiananmen incident, either at home or abroad; some had returned to China for a time but had left again because of problems there. People who failed to readjust to China have no doubts that they cannot live in China as it is. One person feared returning because people he had attacked during the Cultural Revolution were now in control of his home unit. Some of these people did express an interest in returning to China to get involved in politics, but only after major changes have occurred would they think about returning.

These people are also more secure in their ability to stay in the United States, either because they have a green card (12 percent of this group) or citizenship, because they expect to get a "June 4 green card" (i.e., permanent residence status under the presidential executive order of April 1990), or because they have stable jobs. Several also knew that the successes they were having in research in the United States could not be duplicated under China's current conditions, either because of a lack of equipment or limited funding, so they said they were not likely to return.

Group 7: Definitely will not go back

In most cases some critical event has left the 7.3 percent who "definitely will not go back" with personal animosity toward China or the Chinese Communist Party. One person vowed that "even if they threaten to kill me, I will not return." These people were themselves attacked during the Cultural Revolution, had parents who were attacked at that time, or had parents who had been labeled as "class enemies" or counterrevolutionaries during some earlier campaign. Perhaps they had problems with their home unit or were afraid that their "enemy" there could still find them and hurt them even if they switched units, as they were in the same professional field.

Another type of non-returnee had already resettled once in China but after getting out again now refuses to go back. For example, in one case a fellow went back after getting a master's degree in the United States. He had been persuaded to return in part by promises from the Chinese consulate in New York, which held a party for him and promised him all kinds of benefits if he returned, including a job at a unit under the Chinese Academy of Sciences in Beijing. Upon his return, however, his unit gave him no housing and told him that if the New York consulate promised him something, they should arrange it. The next chance he got to go out, he stayed, and he now believes that people like himself who return to China are stupid.[14]

---

[14] See "Liu si jie yu hui guo ri."

FOUR

Background Characteristics and People's Views about Returning

This chapter addresses two issues: the effect of people's background characteristics and the key role played by major variables such as family, professional advancement, economics, and politics. We will show how key characteristics of our sample—such as their sex, age, class or family background, and city of origin—all can affect who does or does not stay, and why. We will also examine the key considerations that determine what choices these people make. Our analysis involved three stages: first we did bivariate analysis, looking to see if the relationship between background variables and the decision to return was significant. If that finding was not significant, we also looked to see if one background variable had a stronger effect than another for any of the seven groups discussed above. Finally, based on variables that appeared to have an important bivariate relationship, we built a model of the key variables that we believed most strongly affected people's overall decision on staying or returning. Using this latter technique, and employing a statistical method called logistic regression analysis, we evaluated the effect of all the key variables at the same time; this analysis and evaluation gives us a much more reliable and powerful explanation of what factors lead people to think of returning than does the simpler bivariate analysis.[1]

Family Background

As in the studies by Glaser and El-Saati, family background helped explain who is getting out, who is likely to stay, and who is thinking seriously about going home. Children of intellectuals (i.e., people who work in universities) made up a very large proportion of our total group, suggesting that they have greater access to overseas education than other

---

[1] For a longer discussion of the logistic regression analysis, see appendix B.

groups in China. Clearly this social group has been allocating an enormous number of these opportunities to their own offspring, a practice that can only bode ill for scholarly and scientific developments on the mainland, given that members of this social group tend to be more alienated from the political system and therefore are more likely to stay in the United States than are the children of workers or peasants. Thus while overall there is no significant statistical tie between family background and views about returning, the percentage of people with peasant or worker background returning to China is greater than their share of the overall population, suggesting that some greater degree of loyalty is at work: children of workers, for example, though only 9.5 percent of the total population, made up 18.2 percent of those definitely returning and 13.6 percent of those in category 2. Similarly, while peasants were only 7.7 percent of the sample, they made up 18.2 percent of those definitely going back and 10.6 percent of those in category 2.[2]

Age

As with the findings of Zhao and Xie, who argued that age was a more significant factor than time spent in the United States in affecting people's views about the Chinese government, we too found that age was important in determining people's views about returning.[3] Also, although people born before 1954 comprised only 27.8 percent of our sample, over 68 percent of them said they were "definitely returning." Similarly, younger people were more likely to fall into the ambivalent category, and they made up a larger percentage of that category than their share of the total sample. Our logistic regression analysis indirectly supports this view as well, as how long people without children had been working in China before they left is a significant factor affecting their decision about returning. Because people without children tend to be younger, and the length of time people worked in China before leaving is also a factor of age, we can suggest that the overall argument that older people who have more long-term ties to China are more likely to return appears to hold true.[4]

---

[2] These findings may reflect the fact that most of the people in category 1 and many in category 2 were visiting scholars, who are older and entered the ranks of high school and university students in the 1950s and 1960s, when there were more channels for upward mobility for peasants and workers.

[3] See Zhao and Xie, "Western Influence." Our chi-square for the relationship between the date of birth and views about returning was significant.

[4] Zhang also found that older people were more likely to return, and when she combined age with year of arrival in the United States to create a new variable, "Age upon arrival in the United States," the correlations with peoples' decisions about returning was

Sex

If we could ask only one question to predict whether people would return, other than their "intentions about returning when they left China," we would want to know their sex. The situation for women in China remains difficult, even though their status is much higher in China than in most of East Asia. Orleans suggests that it was harder for women to get out of China than it was for men. According to Orleans, the percentage of women among government-sponsored J-1 visiting scholars increased from 14 percent in 1979 to 24 percent by 1985, a figure that was slightly lower than the proportion of women in Chinese institutions of higher education. Moreover, among F-1 students, who were mostly self-supporting and therefore not controlled by institutional biases favoring male scholars, the percentage of women was much higher, fluctuating between 37 percent and 45 percent.[5] In our total sample, 29.3 percent were women.

Our findings support the assertion that being a woman significantly affected one's views about returning. First, women are more likely not to want to return than men, with 25.4 percent of women picking categories 6 or 7, while only 14.3 percent of men did so. Also, if we treated responses to question 77 as interval-level data and scaled the responses from 1 (definitely returning and have plans to do so) to 7 (definitely not returning), placing unsure in the middle, then the mean score for men on question 77 was closer to returning (3.4149) than was the mean response for women (3.9873). Thus in our logistic regression analysis, the sex of the respondent is a significant factor for people with children.[6]

Women have less control over their life choices; many more of them than men, for example, came to the United States in the first place to be with their spouses (10 percent of women, compared to 1.04 percent of men). And even among women studying for graduate degrees, the level of those degrees is lower than those attained by the men. While women were equally as likely to get an M.A. as a Ph.D., men were much more likely to get a Ph.D. Thus 23.7 percent of women got M.A.s, as opposed to only 9.4 percent of the men. Similarly, while 26.3 percent of women got Ph.D.s, 47.9 percent of men did so. Women appear to be more concerned about their children's futures and are also more likely to defer to the wishes of their spouses. If husbands want to return, wives tend to

---

even higher. See Zhang, "Residential Preferences," pp. 76–77.

[5] Orleans, *Chinese Students in America,* pp. 96, 98.

[6] The relationship between sex and not returning was significant in multivariate logistic analysis when we used version 1 of question 77, but not when we used version 2.

follow, regardless of their own wishes; but if wives want to return and husbands do not, the couple is likely to stay.

There are also differences between single and married women, with single women being more likely to choose to stay. Comparing married and single women's views about returning, we found that while 28.8 percent of married women picked categories 5–7, 41.7 percent of single women made this choice. These findings support our belief that older single women would be strongly tempted to stay to avoid the social pressures placed on "spinsters," as well as the career limitations placed on women in general (single women are more likely to be career oriented). Individual conversations with women tended to support this view. However, we were surprised to find no overall statistical relationship between a woman's marital status and her views about returning.

Our data suggest several reasons why women are less likely to return. First, women are less confident about their career opportunities in China. While 41 percent of men thought that their career opportunities were "good" to "very good," only 32.5 percent of women felt that way. Second, women tended to be more distrustful of the government's new policies than men. While only 29 percent of men were "uncertain" about the new policies, 38.8 percent of women were. Also, 40 percent of women ranked concerns about political stability as their primary reason for remaining in the United States, while only 27.4 percent of men voiced this as their first concern. Finally, as a good measure of their greater dissatisfaction with life in China, a higher rate of women than men originally intended *not* to return when they left China. Over 10 percent of the women responding to this question left China with the intention of not returning, compared to 5.7 percent of the men.

Several other reasons that did not emerge from the data but that came out in our interviews make women less likely to return. Most women suggested that the conveniences of life in the West—such things as air conditioning, electrical appliances, carpets, the ease with which one can return goods, the level of politeness in shops, the level of cleanliness on the streets and in people's homes—were very important to them. During interviews in their homes, some wives of our respondents argued that the conveniences here are more important to them than the new opportunities in China to make money.

A second key factor is what women called the "complicated nature of human relations," in part a code phrase for the greater constraints imposed upon their behavior and their future by China's traditional political culture. Here it is important to recall El-Saati's assertion that less-personalized performance review systems, which decrease the importance of personal ties in determining promotions, make the West more attractive to people from traditional states who lack connections. This factor seems more important to Chinese women than to Chinese men: whereas men will tolerate the complicated nature of human relations in China in their desire to get ahead, women often mentioned to us how much they hated this part of life in China. But men have reasons not to oppose this system: men are members of the insider networks that affect promotions, and it is men who are in positions of power in the first place. If human relations or links to networks, rather than skills, determine promotions, women are more likely to lose out than men. Also, women are more likely than men to be the targets of sexual innuendo, which is often used to limit promotions in China. Human relations seem simpler in the West, and there seems less need to patronize officials.

Place of Residence in China

The large number of people in our sample who came from Beijing, Shanghai, and Guangdong reflects trends in Chinese educational exchanges with the United States. According to data collected by Orleans on the place of origin of students and scholars in the United States,[7] in 1983–85, Beijingers received 34.3 percent of all J-1 visas and 28.3 percent of all F-1 visas. Shanghaiese, in the same period, received only 15.3 percent of all J-1 visas, but 30.3 percent of F-1 visas. Guangdong, like Shanghai, was able to allocate many fewer central-government-supported opportunities to go abroad than Beijing because Beijing kept control of formal institutional channels in its own hands. But again like Shanghai, Guangdong sent many privately funded students to the United States. While Guangdong averaged only 5 percent of total J-1 visas, it averaged 15 percent of total F-1 visas.

The great number of students in our sample from Beijing, therefore—43.6 percent—is not surprising. In fact, our findings may be slightly skewed away from Beijing because of the high number of students with F-1 or J-1 student visas in our sample. Nevertheless, these findings reflect an enormous inequality of opportunity in that those who live and study in the nation's capital have much better access to overseas study than those who live outside the capital.

These findings on place of residence in China also reflect the enormous bias favoring schools and people who live in the capital or on the coast. While both Wuhan and Chengdu are major centers of academia in China, the percentage of students going overseas from these two cities and their respective provinces is low.[8] Thus of the total number of

---

7 Orleans, *Chinese Students in America*, p. 93.
8 For example, Orleans found that of all F-1 visas, only 2 percent went to people from

people for whom we know the city of origin, 81.2 percent came from coastal cities or provinces (including Beijing).

Relationship to Work Unit in China

One of our key hypotheses was that because the *danwei* played such an important role in people's lives in China—controlling their access to most resources and their official relationships with people outside the unit and outside China—people's attitudes toward their units would be an important determinant of their views on returning. Supervisors control so many aspects of an individual's life in China—including their housing, promotions, and salaries—that bad relations with one's superiors or colleagues greatly limit one's mobility. Therefore, we felt that when respondents said that "politics" affected their decisions, much of the "politics" really reflected the restrictive political culture of their unit.

Our findings both confirmed and refuted this viewpoint. Approximately 75 percent of our respondents reported having "excellent" to "average" relations with their unit leader, so the overall relationship between ties to one's supervisor and views on returning was not statistically significant. However, this relationship is important for the subcategories we created based on responses to question 77. For example, although there is little variation within categories 1–6 about a person's relationship with his or her supervisor (groups 1–6 show a mean score running from 1.46 to 1.74), those who chose number 7 on question 77 and are "definitely not going back" reported having significantly poorer ties with their supervisor (a mean score of 2.4) and are the only people to say that they actually have "bad" ties. Similarly, there was a correlation (significant $p < .03$) between views about superiors and decision to return for those people in categories 2 and 3, who are more likely to go back. This means that having good ties with their superior probably helps them feel positive about returning, even though in the end they still may not return.

Although there is no significant statistical relationship between people's perceptions about their opportunities for promotion in their home unit in China and their views about returning to China, the data

---

Hubei Province, where Wuhan is situated, and less than 1 percent went to those from Sichuan (a province of 110 million people), where Chengdu is situated. However, because the Ministry of Education tried to distribute J-1 visas more evenly, Hubei Province got 4–5 percent of J-1 visas in 1983–85, as did Sichuan Province. On the other hand, well over 80 percent of all F-1 and J-1 visas went to people on the coast. See ibid. In our survey, 4 people (1.8 percent) came from Chengdu.

suggest again that for certain subcategories these two factors are related. For example, those who have decided not to go back (category 7) believe that they have fewer opportunities for promotion than the overall group does.[9] Also, those in categories 1 and 3 ("definitely returning and have plans to do so" and "might go back and have maintained good ties") see greater opportunities for promotion in their home unit than the rest of the population do.

Given the importance of the *danwei* in people's lives, why does it not have a stronger effect on people's views about returning? First, as stated above, most people felt that they had fairly good relations with both their supervisors and their colleagues. And even if relations had been difficult, Chinese people are conditioned to anticipate relatively stormy ties within their work unit. So the absence of serious conflict may be interpreted as "good" ties. Second, because more than half the respondents, including people who were likely to return, were unlikely to return to their home units, relations with people there were not critical to their views about returning. Third, if one already had a *danwei,* one needed its permission to leave China, so the majority of people who left a unit in China probably had good ties with its leaders; otherwise they would not have been able to leave in the first place.

Visa Status and U.S. Government Policy

Chinese government officials and progovernment analysts assert that the U.S. policy to grant permanent residence status to all Chinese who were in the United States as of April 1990 contributed significantly to the brain drain. They argue that if not for that policy, many more people would be returning to China. While in part this assertion is an attempt to deny that the government's own decision to send troops into Beijing led many people to decide to stay,[10] critics may be correct to argue that in the long run more people would return to China if staying in the United States were more difficult. In fact, based on his multivariate analysis, Huang found that the tightening of U.S. immigration policy in 1972 (following a loosening in 1965) and the increased difficulty foreign students had in trying to adjust their status increased the propensity to

---

[9] We compared the mean value responses to this question by the different categories under question 77.

[10] In part, the government had to argue this because it believed it was justified in forcibly ending the Tiananmen protests. Admitting that the deaths in Beijing led people to choose to stay in the United States would be an indirect admission that the military assault on Tiananmen Square had been wrong.

return. Similarly, long waiting periods for status adjustment also pushed people home.[11]

One way to test this hypothesis is to see if there is a significant difference in views about returning among those who came before and after April 1990. The assumption here is that those who came before April 1990 lean toward staying because they are likely to get a green card and therefore would be able to stay, while those who came after April 1990 and are therefore not automatically eligible for a green card are more likely to lean toward returning. Our data show that such a relationship exists.[12] The mean score on returning for those who came before April 1990 was 4.0; for those who came after April 1990, it was 3.0; and for the whole sample, it was 3.59. Thus for people with children, using our logistic regression analysis, the correlation between whether people came before or after April 1990 and their views about returning is significant at the .0292 level (table 11) or at the .0568 level (table 9). Third, another measure of association for these two variables, the chi-square, is highly significant for the entire sample ($p < .000$), showing that when people arrived—that is, before or after April 1990—had an important effect on their views about returning. Finally, dramatic relationships exist for subcategories on the margin. For example, 46.6 percent of our sample came after April 1990. Yet of those people who already had plans to return (category 1), over 90 percent (20 of 22) came after April 1990. No doubt, since people in category 1 are almost all visiting scholars, who are more likely to return in the first place (especially if they came after April 1990), these findings are not convincing. But for other subgroups of the sample the findings are more significant. For example, while the distribution of people's views about returning that fell into categories 2–5 reflects respondents' share of the overall sample population, over 85 percent of people in category 6 (23 of 27) and 90 percent of people in category 7 (17 of 20; i.e., the people who are least likely to return) came before April 1990. While this finding may reflect that people who have been here longer favor staying and have been able to make the necessary arrangements to do so, regardless of their visa status, few people who came after April 1990, and who therefore are not automatically eligible for the green card, probably believed that they had a real chance to stay. So, when asked, they admitted that they would probably return. Thus, while 27.3 percent of our sample leaned toward staying

---

[11] See Huang, "Empirical Analysis," p. 240.

[12] Several versions of the logistic regression analysis strongly support the argument that April 1990 is a critical factor in people's decision about staying or returning. See tables 8, 9, and 11.

(total of categories 5–7), only 15.5 percent of those people came after April 1990.

To what extent did the visa that a person came under affect his or her ability to stay in the United States? Our findings suggest that the visa that people came under had some effect, but not a very significant one. Why? First, most people who came on F-1 student visas (at whatever time) are still on that visa because F-1 visas are easy to extend. Second, under President Bush's Executive Order 12711 (see appendix D), people who came to the United States before April 1990 were legally able to change their visa status from the more restrictive J-1 visa—which would have forced them to return to China for two years after their studies (for J-1 student visas), their research, or their teaching was completed—to the more liberal F-1 visa, which allows them to stay in the United States indefinitely. Significant numbers of people availed themselves of this opportunity to jettison the J-1 visa. This way, they could remain even if no formal law had been enacted to allow all Chinese students and scholars in the United States the chance to stay. Visiting scholars changed their visas in several ways: 22.7 percent of people who came as J-1 visiting scholars changed to F-1 visa status, 9.1 percent got work permits (H-1 visas), 4.5 percent got J-1 student visas, and 10.6 percent got permanent residence status. In the end, only 54.5 percent of people in our sample who came on a J-1 visiting scholar visa were still in the United States on that visa, which means that for the other 44.5 percent of people, the visa they came on had no effect on whether or not they would be able to stay in the United States. Similarly, there was significant movement among those who arrived under a J-1 student visa. Of those who came on J-1 student visas, which were used more freely after 1987 to force junior faculty in China to return, 29 of 51 shifted out of that category: 6 (11.8 percent) got an H (temporary worker) visa, 7 (13.7 percent) achieved permanent resident status, 2 (3.9 percent) had become U.S. citizens, and 14 (27.5 percent) had shifted to F-1 student status. Thus, of all J-1 visas, 50.5 percent changed their status without having to return home for two years.

One surprising trend is the relative ease with which current J-1 visa holders are able to shift to F-1 student visas. According to the policy of the United States Information Agency (USIA), if a Chinese J-1 visa holder can get a "no objection letter," in the form of a legal note from the Chinese embassy or consulate, the USIA will authorize a shift of status. According to several reports, the Chinese embassy in Washington is freely giving out these letters to those who make the request. As a result, the role of the J-1 visa in constraining the brain drain has declined.

Field of Study

Studies of the brain drain suggest that field of specialization may affect people's decisions about returning, although Glaser suggests that it plays a role for only a few fields.[13] Thus we were not surprised to find no overall significant statistical relationship between field of study and views on returning. However, as we analyzed this issue in greater depth, we discovered some interesting facts.

First, there are significant variations among the different fields in terms of views about returning. Of all fields (whose mean score on question 77 was 3.57), those in the applied social sciences, such as law and economics, were the most likely to return (mean score of 2.76), while those in the humanities and arts were least likely to return (mean of 3.81). People in the natural and applied sciences, however, who can get good jobs in both societies, displayed no special trend.[14] Thus we would anticipate that they might be more ambivalent about returning than most other groups. The data, however, show that they are only slightly more ambivalent than their share of the population would indicate (60 percent of the sample, 69.8 percent of the "ambivalent" [category 4]). Social scientists, too, are in a dilemma, so returning or staying is no easy choice. Jobs in the United States are hard to come by, except for those who have graduated from a top school. But the political constraints on what social scientists write and their low salaries in China are more serious problems for them than for those in other fields. For example, one recipient of a Ford Foundation grant doing research on Latin America expects to stay for some time, partly because his wife likes life in the United States. However, he realizes that it will not be easy for him to compete in the United States as a specialist on Latin America, so he does not anticipate that he can stay forever unless he changes his field, which he hesitates doing.

Thus a new trend among Chinese social science Ph.D.s in the United States is to move to universities in Hong Kong. There they can find higher salaries and greater academic freedom than in China but still live in a Chinese culture and have opportunities to visit China frequently.

---

[13] Glaser found that those in languages, education, architecture, and several of the biological sciences were most likely to stay abroad, while those in business, agriculture, and philosophy were more likely to return. See Glaser, *Brain Drain,* pp. xi–xii.

[14] For a few scientific fields there are severe limitations overseas because of issues of security clearance. For example, nuclear engineers will probably go back because concerns over secrecy in the United States make it impossible for them to get jobs in their field. We interviewed a few in Albuquerque who said that they knew they would have to return; nevertheless, they too were planning to put off returning for some time in order to earn money before going home.

For example, three Chinese who had received Ph.D.s at universities in the Boston area, with degrees in sociology, anthropology, and education, had all gone initially to universities in Hong Kong. Whether this trend will continue is hard to predict, as some of these scholars feel that mainlanders are looked down upon in Hong Kong.[15]

Finally, because it is easier to find employment in some fields than in others, we wondered if people tried to change their field of study as a strategy for staying in the United States. While only 29 (10.6 percent of our sample) changed fields, 48.3 percent shifted into the applied sciences and 24.1 percent switched into business, suggesting that this immigration strategy was at work. For example, after the wife of one Ph.D. student in Buffalo received her M.A. in English, she returned to college to become a nurse. She, far more than her husband, is adamant about not returning, and getting a job as a nurse is an important step toward securing her future abroad.[16]

---

[15] Of those three, one has since taken a job in China; one has returned to the United States, feeling that Hong Kong people looked down on mainlanders; and the third has remained in Hong Kong.

[16] In the early 1980s, some women who went to Chicago's Loop College to study English switched into nursing, a change that allowed them to find a job and stay. In fact, according to Orleans, in 1983–85, Loop College, hardly a household name in the United States, had the tenth-largest number of PRC F-1 students of any college in the United States. See Orleans, *Chinese Students in America*, p. 106. This college became an important channel for potential migrants from China to enter the United States.

FIVE

Why People Do Not Return

This chapter addresses four broad factors—the family, economic concerns, political concerns, and desires for personal advancement—to see what role they play in people's decision about whether or not to return. While these four factors may be seen as competing hypotheses, all of them may play some role in affecting people's decisions about returning. The crucial detail is to determine which factors are more important and why.

To assess the effect of these factors we asked various closed-ended questions about why people might return, why they might stay, and what they liked and did not like about the United States. The list of possible responses was based both on our own insights and on conversations with Chinese students and scholars in Toronto. For each question we asked people to pick their three most important choices, and we then ranked their answers to assess what people saw as the key reasons for their own behavior and the behavior of others. The responses to these questions are listed in tables 2 through 5.

To ensure that the expressed views more closely reflected people's intended behavior, we isolated the reasons for returning chosen by those people in categories 1–3, who were leaning toward returning (table 6). Similarly, we isolated the views about *not* returning chosen by people in categories 5–7, who are leaning toward staying (table 7). We deliberately did not ask them to take a position on an issue that does not motivate them and about which they may not have had a real opinion because that would move us even further from the realm of behavior into the realm of hypothesis. Nevertheless, tables 6 and 7 show that even people *not* leaning in a particular direction were in touch with the factors that were motivating people who *were* leaning in that direction. Thus when we compare the rankings of the different explanations about why people did or did not return chosen by the entire sample (tables 2 and 3) to those explanations chosen by people who were or were not leaning toward returning (tables 6 and 7), the final rankings of the reasons for returning or not do not change very much. Thus even if people were not returning themselves, they had a pretty good sense about why others might return, and vice versa.

Finally, drawing on a list of variables that showed some significant bivariate relationship with question 77 (views about returning), we built a more complex model and then, using logistic regression analysis, tested it against the views about returning. Through this methodology we are able to evaluate the independent role of each factor, all the while taking into account the effect that all the other variables in the model are also having on the decision to return or not.

Family Factors

Certain family factors might affect the decision to return, including parental views about returning, concerns for children, and the attitude of one's spouse about returning.

China is a Confucian society, where filial piety remains an important value. Therefore, we asked people about their parents' views of their staying overseas and whether or not their parents' views affected their decision about returning (see figure 6). Of the 257 people who responded to this question, 29.9 percent reported that their parents either "strongly wanted them to stay" (11.6 percent) or "wanted them to stay" (18.3 percent). A plurality of 45.1 percent reported either that their parents "did not care" what they did or that they were "unsure" about their parents' views. Only 17.9 percent said that their parents wanted them to come home, and 7.0 percent reported that their parents "strongly" wanted them to come home. The findings that many parents wanted their children to stay overseas is not surprising. Reports from China suggest that many parents see having children overseas as a status symbol and as a way for other members of the family to get out.[1] For these families, getting a child overseas may be part of a family strategy of diversifying risk—families may decide that it is best to have one child in North America and one in China—or it may be the first step to having the family emigrate out of China.

Why did people's parents hold these views? The betrayal experienced by the generation of intellectuals who returned in the 1950s and who suffered during the Cultural Revolution leads some to push their grown children to stay overseas. Thus one person we interviewed who came to the United States in the mid-1980s was pressured by his mother to break off with his mainland girl friend and marry a Taiwanese girl

---

[1] For a discussion of parents' attitudes toward having children overseas, see Ren Donglai, "Popular Images."

born in the United States to ensure eligibility for U.S. citizenship. Although he was often invited to return to China, his parents, who were high-ranking professors, strongly objected to his returning because they had returned in the early-1950s after studying in the United States and had suffered for doing so.

Economics may lead parents to press their children to stay overseas. Of our 273 respondents, 212 (77.7 percent) reported that they were helping their family back home in some significant way: 18.7 percent were bringing a family member to the United States, 7.3 percent were sending back goods that were hard to buy in China, 42.9 percent were giving financial support, 0.7 percent (two people) were helping them buy a house, and 8.1 percent were helping in other, unspecified ways. Given these data, we should not be surprised to find that some parents in China did not want their children to return.

Yet despite their concerns, people's parents had influence in only a few cases. Of the 255 people who responded to this question, 81.9 percent reported that their parents' view had "only a little influence" (38.8 percent) or "no influence at all" (43.1 percent), while only 3.1 percent reported that their parents had "a great deal of influence" on their decision about returning. One U.S. Ph.D. we interviewed in China said that he had returned primarily because his parents were in ill health, and he was an only child.

The status of one's spouse, however, is an important factor in the decision to return. In our sample, 205 people had been married, 59 had never married, and 10 were divorced (nine cases were missing). Of the 205 married people, only 39 had not brought their spouses to the United States. While the relationship between being married and views of returning was not statistically significant, whether the spouse was in the United States was.[2] Moreover, the mean scores on question 77 for these two groups—married people with spouses here and those whose spouses were not here—are significantly different. Those people whose spouses are still in China are much more inclined to return than the entire population, especially when they are compared to people whose spouses are already here. Thus, while the mean score for the entire sample on returning to China was 3.585, the mean score for people with spouses in China was 2.615, while for those whose spouses are here it was 3.831.

These findings support our general observations that a major attitude shift occurs among Chinese students and scholars once they get their spouse out. For example, one Tufts student who had been adamant about returning to China quickly changed his plans and moved to Canada

---

[2] The chi-square was significant at .00002.

after his wife arrived. Clearly, keeping spouses in China increases the probability that scholars and students will return.

In light of these findings, it is surprising that the U.S. and Chinese governments softened the restrictions that limited the availability of F-2 and J-2 visas for spouses, thereby making it easier for spouses to come to the United States. According to Orleans, before 1984 few spouses got these visas—fewer than a hundred J-2 and F-2 visas had been issued by that time—but the number increased in 1984 (412) and then ballooned in 1985 (2,274) and in 1986 (2,581).[3] It was around this time, too, that people became less inclined to go back. Given our findings, that once the spouse arrives the probability of returning decreases significantly, we can see that the decision to open the gates to the United States to spouses of students has contributed significantly to the brain drain that has followed.

Did a spouse's dissatisfaction with life in the United States affect the decision to return? Overall, we did not find that respondents' views concerning their spouses' attitudes about being here were significant. For the most part, the men called the shots. If the wife wanted to return but the man did not, the family was likely to stay; if the husband wanted to return, however, the family was more likely to go back. Nevertheless, we did find that people in category 2 ("definitely going back but don't know when") had the highest mean score in terms of spouse's dissatisfaction about being in the United States. Perhaps it is the wife's dissatisfaction that leads these people to say that they are definitely going back, even though other factors are drawing them to stay. Thus they say that they are definitely going back, but they also cannot say when.

One would have assumed that if the spouse wants to leave, the student or visiting scholar would be pressured to go back. However, because we did not interview the spouses, we have no data on the effect of the spouse's views. We did ask whether people thought their spouse supported their view about returning, and not surprisingly there is a remarkably strong relationship between views about returning and a person's perception of her or his spouse's current views about whether or not they should remain. For example, 6 of 10 people whose spouse strongly wants them to come home were going back,[4] while none of the people who said that their spouse strongly wanted them to stay were even considering going back. Similarly, of the 39 people whose spouse strongly wanted them to stay, 46 percent (18) were very unlikely to

---

³ Orleans, *Chinese Students in America*, p. 96.

⁴ Thus while the percentage of people whose spouse strongly wanted them to come home was only 3.7 of the total population, those whose spouse strongly wanted them to come back and who were going back made up 27.3 percent of all returnees in category 1.

return or were definitely not returning, while only 23 percent (9) were even considering going back. Moreover, only 1 was on his way back. The measure of association we used for the spouse's current view about the interviewee's returning and the interviewee's own views about returning, our multiple regression, showed an R^2 of .269 with an extremely high probability. No doubt this finding reflects people's desires to see their spouse supporting their own decision, but similarity of views on these issues among married people would not be surprising.

One reason people were not returning was that individuals feel pressure from their families and friends to get permanent residence status. According to our respondents, "You get a degree for yourself, but you get the green card for others"—for your relatives, parents, children, and friends. Thus, one person from Fujian who wanted to go back to China said that he was criticized by his entire family in China and by many of his friends who felt that if he had a chance to get permanent residency, he should not consider going back. Another person had not applied for a green card until he visited China and found his friends incredulous that he hadn't. He then returned to the United States and has since received permanent residency.

We also hypothesized that people's attitudes about their children's schooling might affect their views about returning. The number of Chinese in our sample who already have their children with them in the United States is remarkable, a testament to the openness of both U.S. and Chinese society. Thus of the 136 people with children in our sample, 62.8 percent have their children with them in the United States.

The data on the effect that plans for children's schooling has on views about returning are complex. Having children in the United States is only slightly related to views about returning (R^2 of .13), because people have different views about their children's schooling. Over 38 percent of people with children in the United States prefer that their children go back to China for primary education; one person was afraid that his child would take up drugs and gambling in the United States. So concerns about their children's public school education actually pulls them home. On the other hand, 74 percent of the people with children whom we interviewed want their children to stay in the United States for college. This factor, therefore, motivates them to stay in the United States (the chi-square is significant), as only by staying and earning an income here can they ensure that their children will have the opportunity to study in the United States.[5] Yet the multiple regression R^2 was only

---

[5] The overall mean score on returning (question 77) for people's views about the children's college education was 3.56. For those who want their children to go to college in the United States, the mean was 4.06, while for those who want their children to go to

.03. Similarly, this variable was not significant in our logistic analysis. Thus, while these two variables move in tandem, other, more powerful, factors are influencing the relationship.

For example, a visiting scholar who went to a university in Boston in 1992 decided to move to Toronto primarily because he wanted to get his son into a university in Canada. He had come to the United States under a grant given to his research institute in China from a foundation in Hong Kong, but from the beginning he had been looking to get his son out of China and into a school in the West. His actions are a problem for his institute, as the rules of his fellowship stipulate that if the recipient does not return, his unit can never get the grant again. His unit wants him at least to pay back the grant money, but he was resisting this demand as well. This case shows that it is hard to predict even what visiting scholars will do when their children's future is included in their calculation and especially after their children have already left China.

Yet the bivariate relationship between our interviewees' plans for their child's primary or college education and their own views about returning to China is not very strong when we examine whether other factors are affecting their views about returning. For example, when we asked our respondents why people might return, very few people chose "better education for my children." In part, this finding may reflect the poor quality of university education in China; but public school education in China remains of a high quality, and 38.4 percent of people with children were planning to send them to primary school in China. Similarly, when asked what people liked most about the United States, only 3.3 percent chose "a better future for my children" on the first round. Moreover, when we include these factors in our multivariate logistic analysis, the effect of people's plans for either their children's public school or university education is not statistically significant (see table 8). Clearly, such other factors as political freedom, economic improvement, and personal development were more important influences on people's views about returning than was their children's educational future.

Personal Development

Personal development comprises many factors, including the ability to choose career paths or research topics, to gain access to advanced research facilities, and to maximize one's social status. State constraints on job choice or areas of specialization, which are only beginning to break down, led us to wonder if the work environment in China, the

---

in China, the mean score on returning was 2.29.

limits on mobility, and the extent to which relocating to the United States improved people's work environment would influence our interviewees' decisions about staying in the United States. According to Glaser, young people's concerns over the constraints on life choices in traditional, hierarchical societies or the lack of appropriate jobs in the home country push people out. Given the highly authoritarian nature of Chinese society, the motivations cited by Glaser should be important to the many young Chinese who uprooted themselves and moved to the United States to improve their lives, particularly if they had no children.

We approached this issue in a variety of ways. First we tried to determine the career status of people in our sample. Were they already upwardly mobile in China, or were they frustrated in their careers and looking to get out? Our findings show that many people were well positioned in China, and while they may have left for career advancement, they did not feel particularly constrained in China. Thus 56.3 percent of respondents believed that they had "excellent" (17 percent) or "good" (39.3 percent) opportunities for promotion within their unit. Similarly, 11.3 percent of respondents believed that they had "very good" opportunities for developing their abilities within their home unit, while another 33.1 percent felt that they had "relatively good" opportunities. Only 22.6 percent felt that they had "very little" or "no opportunity for personal development" within their former unit. Thus, many of these people are not escapees from an environment in which they have no future; at least half are talented people who had many opportunities in China but chose to improve their life chances by going abroad. Still, they might still have felt somewhat constrained by the lack of job mobility.

Second, did career issues motivate people to think about staying overseas? The responses to question 88, which poses several plausible reasons why people might not return to China, are given in table 3 and show that, when offered these choices, many people chose career-related reasons for not returning to China. For 10.6 percent of the people we interviewed, "lack of career advancement" was the first reason for not returning to China and was the third most important reason overall. Also, if one combines all responses reflecting career issues, 32.2 percent of the people interviewed chose factors related to personal development.[6]

---

[6] These included lack of opportunity to change jobs in China, lack of opportunity for career advancement in China, poor work environment in China, lack of modern equipment for one's research or work, lack of suitable jobs given one's education and training, and lack of contact or exchanges with international scholars in one's field.

Among factors that structure concerns about opportunities for personal development, the sex of the respondent is quite important. Although 41 percent of the men felt that their "opportunities within their unit to develop their abilities" were "very good" to "relatively good," only 32.5 of the women felt that way.

Issues of personal development led some people to prefer the United States to China. When asked to choose three positive things about the United States and to rank them, the second most common response was "lots of job choices or opportunity"; "good working conditions" ranked third (see table 4). Among those people who were leaning toward not returning (categories 5–7 on question 77), "lots of job opportunities" was the second most important strength of the United States. Thus, job mobility and the constraints of China's manpower system are powerful forces leading people to stay.

But personal development is a two-sided issue, leading some people to think about returning home as well. Given the relatively high status of this group in China before they left, our interviewees chose "higher social status in China" (and not patriotism) as the most important reason why people might return to China.[7] This fact was true both for the entire sample population and for people who were leaning toward returning to China. Similarly, for the whole sample, "better career opportunities in China" was the second most popular reason for returning. Also, many of our interviewees expressed serious worries about racism in the United States, a concern directly related to social status. When Chinese in the United States feel that they are granted low social status, they do not see their lowly position as the natural status of immigrants; rather, they inevitably attribute their low status to an anti-Chinese bias in the United States. Thus one professor we interviewed in Sichuan Province in 1992 had returned to China because of what he saw as anti-Chinese racism: His academic sponsor at a university in California had asked him to supervise some graduate students. One was a Korean student whose university stipend was higher than the one the professor received from the same university. Although the professor told us that he saw this as racism, in many ways he was responding to the low social status he had in the United States. Once he returned to China, he became an assistant professor, a position that gave him greater status and respect.

---

[7] Based on his qualitative interviews, Brzezinski found that "honor," "prestige," and "respect" were three of the most important and prevalent themes motivating his six respondents to go to university and then migrate to the United States. See Brzezinski, *Migration and Opportunity*, p. 9. Yet these same themes often propel older scholars back to China.

Another issue related to personal development is the ability to control one's own research. Chinese spend many years in research labs doing analysis for their research director, who sets their research agenda. Thus those who can direct a lab in China but are forced to work for others here in the United States may choose to return to China.[8] Anecdotal data suggest that talented people who cannot get jobs or research positions in the West where they are their own boss or where they can propose their own research projects are more likely to go back. For example, the Canadian supervisor of a Chinese scholar in London, Ontario, would not let him publish articles in his own name or go to conferences to present his own work. The Canadian professor insisted on presenting the work himself—not an uncommon situation in China. However, this scholar felt that in the Canadian context, he should be allowed to present his own work. In 1993, he was trying to decide whether to stay in Canada but cut off ties with this professor or simply go home.

Economic Variables

A critical assumption behind this study was that in 1993, four years after Tiananmen, economics, more than politics, would be the driving force behind many people's decisions about not returning to China.[9] We believed that as people compared their current or anticipated economic situation in the United States to their potential economic situation in China, they would decide that the economic gap was too great and so would opt to stay. We believed that as the political aftershock of Tiananmen receded, economics would be the most important determinant. We believed that if people's economic conditions in the United States were really disastrous, more might consider going back, especially if economic conditions in China improved. As we look at the data, we cannot say that economics is *the* most important factor; nevertheless, it looms very large in people's calculations about staying in the United States.

---

[8] There are few opportunities to open new labs or become project directors in the major research centers in China. People would find it necessary to go to inland cities, which Orleans argues people do not want to do. They would prefer to stay in the United States, working in less prestigious positions, than return to parts of China other than coastal cities.

[9] Zhang dissented from economic explanations, which she claimed were the core view of the mainstream brain drain literature (Zhang, "Residential Preferences," p. 11). She felt that for cultural reasons, including traditional negative views about people who seek wealth, Chinese people, especially after the Tiananmen incident, were far more likely to be motivated by political reasons than by " 'higher pay and better living conditions,' which ha[ve] been identified as the primary contributors to the brain drain" (p. 17).

We first sought data about peoples' economic conditions in the United States under the assumption that if people were doing well, they were more likely to stay. First, we found that conditions were mixed; some people were living rather well, while others were just scraping by. But perceptions often were better than the real conditions. For example, when we looked at people's housing, we found that only 7.7 percent owned their own housing, and only 21.6 percent lived in anything as large as a two-bedroom apartment. The others (66.3 percent) lived in a one-bedroom apartment (29.7 percent) or a studio (21.6 percent) or shared a room in a house or apartment (15 percent). The mean rent people were paying was $390.00. Yet when asked how they would compare their housing in the United States to their housing in China, 39.2 percent saw their housing as "much better," while another 26.0 percent thought their housing was "a little better." Thus almost two-thirds of our sample believed that they had improved their housing.

In terms of total family income, the Chinese students and scholars in our sample are doing relatively well, with a mean income of $20,000–$25,000 per family (see figure 2). Of the 262 cases for which we have data, 20.9 percent of the sample's total household income was less than $10,000 and another 32.4 percent earned $10,000–$20,000. Therefore, almost half (46.7 percent) of the households in our sample made more than $20,000, with 32.4 percent of the sample earning pretax total household incomes of more than $25,000. As the sample includes a significant number of single graduate students who are getting by on part-time jobs, as well as families who are relying on the labor of one adult while the other goes to school full time, this group is doing quite well and has strong economic incentives for staying in the United States.[10] Moreover, when asked to describe their "overall living standard," 52 percent thought that it was "good" (38.8 percent) or "excellent" (13.2 percent), 37.4 percent that it was "average," leaving just over 10 percent who felt that it was "comparatively poor" or "very poor." When asked to compare their "overall economic situation" in the United States to their "economic situation in China," 34.1 percent thought that their situation was "much better," another 35.2 percent that it was "a little better." Still, almost one-third did not think that their economic situation in the United States was better than it had been in China.

Economic factors varied by region in our sample. Regarding housing, people in California were most likely to own their own housing, even though the people interviewed in New York were almost all out in

---

[10] One must recall that the poverty line in the United States is approximately US$14,000 for a family of four.

the workforce. Similarly, people in Albuquerque and California more often saw their current housing as significantly better than their housing in China, while New York and Boston residents did not describe as great an improvement. Regarding income, people in Buffalo were the poorest, perhaps in part because it is a border town, and therefore wives on H-2 or J-2 visas find it harder to get jobs. However, Buffalo is also in a more depressed part of the United States, so very few people worked off campus. People in Albuquerque tended toward middle-income levels, while people from New York were the richest in our sample (as noted above, almost all were already in the workforce). When asked to compare their overall living standards in the United States against those in China, people in California and Albuquerque again had a more positive view of their situation in the United States than did people in New York, Boston, and Buffalo.

The logistic regression analysis confirmed the importance of economic determinants as a factor affecting people's decision to stay. Yet their importance varied depending on whether or not people had children. For people with children, the comparison of their housing in the United States to that in China was a very strong explanation for their decision to stay, with a level of significance of .0006 (see table 8).[11] Given the poor condition of most people's housing in China, and given that nearly 30 percent of people in our sample now lived in a two-bedroom apartment or better, the finding that better housing is motivating people to stay in the United States is not surprising. Especially when compared to China, where a couple with a child often live in a one-bedroom apartment, housing in the United States must seem spacious, offering parents a level of privacy unavailable in China.

For people without children, real household income in the United States and "overall economic situation" looms large in their decision to stay (table 10). While housing is not important for them—they may not have a spouse who cares about better housing or children who increase the importance of space—both their total pretax household income and their comparison of their "overall economic situation" now in the United

---

[11] In our second modeling of these explanations, where we excluded the effect of people's views about their children's education (see table 9), the effect of comparing housing in the United States with China was still significant at the .0012 level. Also, when we employed another method, which we call "version 1" (see appendix C), for measuring our dependent variable (the answer to question 77) and removed the effect of parental plans for children's education from the model, views about housing are no longer significant, but household income is (.04), even for people with children (see table 11). Thus, regardless of which model we use, economics is a statistically significant factor affecting the decision of people with children about whether or not to return to China.

States to that in China are significant factors explaining their views about staying or returning. According to our logistic regression, the probability chi-square for these two variables was .0068 and .0428, respectively. Age may also be at work here, as people without children are probably younger and therefore may have lived with eight other students in a university dorm before leaving China. Still, views on housing were not as important for this group.

Yet although these findings are not as strong as we might have anticipated—in that some of the economic variables were not significant[12]—even people whose incomes had not improved (17.9 percent) or had gotten worse (7.3 percent) may have anticipated better economic conditions in the near future. For example, one person we interviewed in Toronto had looked for work without success for two years; despite great difficulties, he did not want to return to China, believing that he would soon find a good job. He is now selling insurance, and his income is much better than it would be in China.

On the other hand, China's improved economy and the U.S. recession that was still at work in early 1993, when we conducted many of our interviews, are leading a small number of people to return to China. However, we believe that this trend affects mostly people from high-ranking families. For example, one Harvard Ph.D. student in urban planning from a southern province felt that he had lost out economically by going overseas. Many of his friends in China were making lots of money doing business, while he, a poor student, had to work in a low-level job (*da gong*) off campus to pay his living expenses. He believes he is much worse off than his friends; moreover, since he comes from a relatively high ranking family, he could make a lot of money in China. Nevertheless, he plans to finish his studies, as he recognizes that in the China of the future a Harvard Ph.D. may be quite valuable. One of his friends in Boston, who comes from a high-ranking military family, has a brother and sister involved in the steel and auto business in China. The friend came to the United States through a third country, having worked there as an agent for a Chinese company headquartered in Shenzhen, China's most prosperous Special Economic Zone. After arriving in the United States, he quit school and has earned almost US$300,000 doing business. As soon as he gets his green card he will return to China

---

[12] When asked to choose "positive things about America," "higher standard of living" ranked fifth as people's first choice, but it ranked second and first as their second and third choices respectively. Also, for most of our models of the logistic regression analysis (tables 8 and 9), "household income" and "comparing overall situation now to that in China" were not significant factors affecting choices about returning for people with children.

because, as a U.S. permanent resident, he will be able to travel back and forth freely and will be treated in China as an "overseas Chinese."

One fellow, whose situation was described in the dissident publication *Democratic China,* had not planned to return when he left China, but after graduating with a degree in business, he changed his mind. While the U.S. economic recovery was slow, China presented a big market and, because there were as yet few government regulations, lots of opportunity for making money. He was excited by the reports of people who were making money on land speculation, but he also realized that as the legal framework in China tightened, it would become harder to make money there. So he wanted to return quickly to make money while it was easy to do so. Similarly, the son of a high-ranking official was nervous that so many people were making so much money in China. Although he and his wife were already earning middle-class salaries in the United States, he knew that with his contacts he could make much more money back in China. He is now working for an American company in Beijing.

That Chinese are pulled to the United States and desire to stay here for many of the same reasons as other national groups—including to improve their economic situation—should not be surprising: there are serious economic reasons for Chinese to want to remain in the United States. Chinese scholars in our sample, including postdoctoral fellows, are doing well financially. For people with children, better housing is a strong pull. For those without children, total household income and the comparison of their economic situation in China to their situation in the United States are strong forces keeping them here. We accept that in 1989, soon after Tiananmen, respondents in the surveys cited previously almost unanimously picked politics as the key factor affecting their choices about returning. Given the salience of politics in 1989–90, in the wake of Tiananmen, any other findings would be suspicious. Moreover, as we will see, even four years after Tiananmen, political factors remain more important than we had originally anticipated. But as the drama of Tiananmen and the salience of those events receded somewhat, the desire for economic betterment became a more important factor at work among our sample. That economics is an important motivating factor for some people is also indicated by the fact that as business opportunities emerge in China, those who are well positioned to gain from them—the well-connected Chinese who care little about political factors—are now looking for ways to return and profit from China's booming economy.

Political Reasons

While we assumed that economics was more important than politics, many Chinese in the United States strongly believe that dissatisfaction with the Chinese government is the most important reason people do not return. In studies done immediately after June 4, 1989, political anger and hostility toward the regime did emerge as the key factors. Even when given the chance to choose economic reasons for not returning, Chinese in a number of surveys carried out in the wake of Tiananmen consistently chose political factors. Yet, as we have shown above, since Tiananmen, economics has emerged as an important variable, pushing politics somewhat into the background. Nevertheless, as this section will show, politics—the desire for political freedom, fears of political instability, lack of trust in the government, and the political experiences of the past forty years—remains a salient factor affecting people's calculations about whether or not to return to China.

We approached the role of politics in the same way that we addressed the other large explanatory variables. Our primary political variables in the data set were responses to questions 92 (the effect of June 4 on decisions whether or not to stay in the United States) and 98 (trust in the Chinese government's promise to let returned scholars travel freely out of China). Figures 7 and 8 show the responses to these two questions. To break down the political element further and facilitate our multivariate analysis, we looked at what percentage of people chose political factors as their reason for not returning (see table 3). To our surprise, "lack of political stability" was by far the most common reason people gave for not returning.[13] Far more people made it their first choice than any other reason.[14] Also, when we combine those who chose "lack of political stability" with those who chose "lack of political freedom" (12.4 percent), 42.7 percent of those who responded chose political concerns as their main reason for not returning.

We also built a political variable by combining a number of political issues, then tested it in our logistic regression analysis.[15] This composite political variable proved to be significant for the cohort with children

---

[13] Some Chinese who worked on our study expressed concerns that politics did not seem to play as large a role as they had anticipated. However, given the salience of political factors that we have discovered, they should feel confident that our findings reflect the real values and drives for a significant percentage of the expatriate community in the United States and Canada.

[14] This finding correlates with much of the literature on the brain drain, which found that "instability" did push people out of the Third World (see Lakshmana Rao, *Brain Drain*, p. 5). However, in the Chinese context, such a finding is relatively political.

[15] Our first political variable combined responses to questions 90–92 and 97–99.

($p<.0556$) and almost significant for those people without children ($p<.1093$) (see tables 8–10). We also tested the effect of politics by using responses to question 88, "why people might not want to return," and differentiating among those who chose "political stability," "political freedom," and any other choice. We also combined people who chose the first two reasons and compared them to the rest of the population. Our findings for this variable show that for people without children, concerns about political stability ($p<.01$) and political freedom ($p<.02$) independently are statistically significant factors determining people's choices about whether to return or to stay. Also, when the people who chose these two responses were combined with people who chose "fear of being arrested," the data show that people without children were clearly influenced by these factors in making their determinations about staying (for those with children, there was no statistical relationship).

Thus we find that younger, less encumbered people are more likely to voice political concerns as key to their decision to stay, while older people with children expressed less concern about either political freedom or political stability. In some ways, the finding that people with children are not strongly motivated by concerns of stability is surprising; however, logistic regression analysis incorporates all the factors that impinge upon the decision. Simply put, for married people with children, mundane concerns such as housing are more important. However, when we measured politics in a different manner and included this political variable in our regression analysis, it was a significant factor for people with children. In our multivariate analysis this "combined political variable," which tapped into the effect of issues such as whether their family suffered during the Cultural Revolution, their reactions to June 4, and their level of trust in the Chinese government, was significantly related to their views about returning (see tables 8 and 9). Thus people with children are political in their calculations; they simply do not express it in their choices for question 88 (see table 3).

However, it is critical to differentiate between these two measures of political attitudes. "Political instability" plagues most developing states regardless of regime type, and Glaser and others see it as an important factor that led people both to leave their homeland and to stay abroad. Clearly, Chinese have valid reasons to be concerned about political stability—61.9 percent of people interviewed said that their family had suffered during the Cultural Revolution, while 14.3 percent said that that suffering had been a "very important" or "somewhat important" factor in their decision about returning to China. People are afraid that their lives will again be disrupted by political campaigns, succession crises, or a general chaos that may ensue after Deng's death. But political instability is not usually the kind of political factor that members of the U.S. Congress allude to when they talk of people not returning to China for political reasons. In fact, the type of political liberalization demanded by the U.S. Congress, at a time of great economic stress in China, may trigger the kind of political instability that our interviewees fear most. While an open, more democratic China may be better for all, the political instability that the transition to democracy is likely to engender will keep many people in our sample from returning.

In our view, "lack of political freedom" reflects the views of people who are not returning to China because of their disaffection with the political regime, not just its inability to guarantee a stable environment in which they can pursue their lives. Thus more than 12 percent of the people we interviewed listed "lack of political freedom" as the primary reason why they might not go back. Some 13.7 percent of those already leaning toward not going back made this their first choice. Yet "fear of being arrested," which was a concern commonly expressed by Chinese students in late 1989 and early 1990 as they lobbied for the Chinese student bill, had very little influence on our sample. Only 3 people (1.1 percent) made it their first choice, and only 6 (2.2 percent) made it their third choice. No one made it their second choice.[16] Unfortunately, we did not ask people if they feared political persecution, which may have been a more common fear than the fear of being arrested. One must wonder whether young Chinese consciously misled Congress in order to secure immigration status or whether the political fears that affected them then have simply dissipated as Tiananmen recedes into the background.

We also tapped into concerns about the stability of policy on letting returned scholars go back and forth freely. In early 1992, to get more people to return, China's government introduced what is known as the "freedom to come and go" policy (*laiqu ziyou*). In our sample, we received 257 valid answers. While 51 percent of people completely trust (11.7 percent) or somewhat trust (39.3 percent) the government to keep its word, 15.2 percent completely mistrust or somewhat mistrust the government, and another 33.8 percent are uncertain that the government will keep this promise. For the two latter groups (49 percent), returning is a difficult decision.

One issue we hoped to address in our study was the effect on returning of China's "political culture," defined in terms of state-determined limitations on economic and political freedoms, as well as on personal

---

[16] Nevertheless, we strongly believe that these fears were overstated as a strategy to get residence status, and our data reinforce that view.

advancement. Such limitations result in large part from the dominance of the work unit. We believed that when Chinese who have come to the West referred to a lack of freedom in China, in many cases they were reflecting the constraints of the *danwei* on their actions.[17] Thus, interspersed within the questionnaire was a host of questions that attempted to tap into that component of China's political system. For example, many of the concerns analyzed in the section under personal development are the result of constraints imposed under China's *danwei* system. These include "lack of opportunity to change jobs," which for 5.5 percent constituted the primary reason for not returning. Also, another 7.0 percent chose "fear of not being able to get out of China a second time" as their second choice. (Only 2.9 percent made it their first choice, while 3.3 percent made it their third choice.)

Yet, as we discussed above, these people had better ties and more positive attitudes toward their work unit than we had anticipated. Only 3.1 percent of the people who reported on their relations with their supervisor felt that those relations were "poor" or "bad," while 85 percent felt that they were good or excellent (probably because many students may not have had a work unit or a supervisor in China before leaving, only 196 people responded to this question). When asked about the positive things in the United States, very few chose "good interpersonal relations on the job"; had their experiences in China been more negative, they might have chosen this option. Similarly, only 14.9 percent of people who responded to the question about personal relationships in their work units said that they had "poor" or "very bad" relations with people in their unit, while 51 percent said that they had "excellent" or "good" relations with people in their unit. This political culture variable is more salient for women, who were less likely than men to see opportunities for promotion in their work unit. But the generally positive view these people held about their work unit explains why we found very little correlation between work unit, or other indicators of political culture, and people's attitudes about returning.

Nevertheless, in individual cases, work units used their tools of control to get people to return. In our sample, 20 of 39 people with a spouse still in China had tried and failed to get the spouse out. While in some cases the U.S. government had refused to grant a visa, in other cases the Chinese unit would not let the spouse go. A school in Wuhan that is aggressive about getting its faculty to return pressured two faculty

---

[17] Brzezinski's respondents stressed that this system of state-allocated jobs was unfair and that it limited their opportunities to use their talents. It was therefore an important reason for their not returning to China. Brzezinski, *Migration and Opportunity*.

members to return. One professor went to a meeting in Canada and found a job; but the school's constant cables and pressure were too much, so he planned to return immediately. Another professor from the same school chose not to do a Ph.D. in England because the school refused to let his wife out. In Toronto we met a Ph.D. from the Chinese Academy of Sciences who was offered a job at the University of Toronto by a Chinese mainlander with a Ph.D. from a U.S. university who now teaches at Toronto. But this fellow's unit wanted 20,000 RMB to let his wife go. Initially, it had denied her the right to leave, but when confronted by Document No. 44, which enunciated the policy of "freedom to come and go," they had to let her go; they decided to charge her money instead.

Politics or Economics? "A Gentleman Does **Not** Discuss Personal Interest"

Our findings have shown that concerns about political stability and the high valuation of the political freedom available in the United States are keeping people there. Yet as these data began to emerge, Professor Chen expressed his concerns that more people were actually concerned by economic issues than appeared in the data, but for cultural reasons of face, they did not want to be seen as rejecting China for their own self-interest. According to Chen, it is a traditional Chinese concept that "a gentleman does not discuss personal interest" (*zhunzi bu yan li*). Justifying their refusal to return on political grounds allows the people we interviewed to shift responsibility for not returning onto the current regime and its policies and thereby avoid accusations of selfishly rejecting their homeland. Professor Chen said that some people who during the formal interview chose political reasons—either "stability" or "freedom"—for staying, suggested in private comments after the interview that economics was more important. Having completed the majority of interviews when we decided to address this issue, we employed the following strategy.

In Albuquerque, Chen concluded each of the 50 interviews with the following additional question: "Some people say that the main reason most people don't return is political reasons; others say it is economic reasons. Which do you think it is?" If we found a considerable number of people saying that others did not return for economic reasons, but they themselves had already chosen political reasons in response to question 88, we could infer that they too were motivated by economics, but did not want to say so. Our findings suggest that this hypothesis may be partly true. Of the 50 people interviewed in Albuquerque, 35 (70 percent) said they believed that the main reason most people did not return was economic, 7 (14 percent) people felt that people did not return primarily for political reasons, and 8 (16 percent) said that it was for both economic and political reasons. Yet almost half the 35 people (16) who said others were not returning for economic reasons had named political instability or political freedom as one of their first two reasons for not returning. Thus it appears possible that while some people assert that others are staying in the United States for economic reasons, they legitimize their own motives by labeling them political.

We also looked at the number of people who said they were not returning for political reasons (i.e., people who chose 1–3 on question 88), to see how they evaluated their economic conditions here vis-à-vis their former situation in China and whether their perceptions were significantly different from the overall sample. If they said that their economic situation was much better here than in China, and if that score was significantly better than the overall sample's views, then their choice of politics as the reason for not returning would be suspect. Again our findings suggest that Professor Chen's concerns may have some validity, as people who chose "political freedom" also felt more positive about their housing and their income here as compared to China than did the sample as a whole.[18] On the other hand, our logistic analysis challenges this line of thinking by showing that people without children who chose political stability or political freedom on question 88 were far less willing to return to China than people who did not choose politics. And while people with children who chose political reasons on question 88 for not returning may not have really been affected by these concerns, politics, as measured by our combined political variable, did have a significant effect on their decision about returning.

In the end, we remain confident that political factors are at work in the Chinese student's and scholar's decision making. While some people value the political freedom in the United States, for the majority of people who express their views in political language, the lack of stability in China, rather than political oppression, is the key force. Similarly, freedom in the United States to chose one's job or to pursue one's career more openly is important as well. However, one should not extrapolate from our findings that the majority of people dissent from the political system in China. Should the economy continue to expand, and should

---

[18] Their mean score on comparing housing here to housing in China (with one "much better" and five "much worse") was 1.613; the population mean was 2.103. Similarly, for comparing incomes here versus incomes in China, their mean score was 1.580 versus a population mean of 1.802.

China survive the post-Deng succession without serious instability, more people may return, even if the regime remains relatively authoritarian. Improved job opportunities, an improved standard of living, and political stability may be enough to get more people to return.

SIX

Evaluating the Brain Drain: The Scale of Loss and Problems of Return

The scale of loss for the countries that suffer a brain drain and the benefits to the United States of these flows can be enormous. One study, which put a price tag on the human capital as well as on the cost of educating and training individuals, asserted that India transferred US$51 billion in human capital to the United States from 1976 to 1985.[1] A less shocking figure in a 1974 report to the U.S. Congress estimated that in 1971, the United States saved approximately $835.5 million (the cost of training emigrants who arrived that year), while in the same year the developing countries lost $326.3 million as a direct result of the brain drain.[2] According to a less reliable source, *The Scientific Potential of America,* published in 1977 in the USSR, from 1972 to 1977 the United States absorbed 220,000 foreign experts and thus saved no less than US$15–20 billion in educational investment and related spending. These figures also represent a net loss to developing countries. While these data may not be totally reliable, they do reflect the enormous benefits the United States has gained from its ability to attract foreign brainpower to its shores. For example, of 42 people living in the United States in 1962 who had won the Nobel Prize in physics and chemistry, 35.7 percent were either born overseas or had moved to the United States after winning the award. Similarly, of the 631 members of the American Academy of Sciences in 1961, 42.2 percent were born overseas or had received their higher education overseas.[3]

Given the exceptionally low return rate in all studies of the Chinese brain drain, China is suffering a significant loss of brainpower. But how great is this loss? If these people are still making contributions to

---

[1] "Third World Loss," *Globe and Mail* (Toronto), 8 April 1991.
[2] Sanchez-Arnau and Calvo, "International Mobility," p. 62.
[3] See Xu Yu, "Macroanalysis of the Brain Drain" (Master's thesis, Xiamen University), p. 3.

China, their families, and their home units, China may benefit from "storing brainpower overseas."[4] The following section will assess the extent of the loss, as well as the potential benefits to China of having so many talented Chinese abroad.

How Great an Investment? How Great a Loss?

One measure of the loss caused by the brain drain is the investment China has made in these non-returnees. Is China losing highly qualified people in whom the state had already made a major investment, or are many of the people going to the United States actually gaining much of their training overseas? According to Chang, despite the fact that the return rate of Taiwanese students studying in the United States has been only 18 percent, the loss is not so great because the vast majority of these people were trained in the United States and therefore reflect a "migration and education" pattern, rather than an exodus of high-class scientists and engineers.[5] One can compare this to India, where a highly developed education system trains many Ph.D.s who are educated at home and then migrate to the developed world. In this case, the loss is much greater. To assess this factor we looked at our interviewees' educational levels when they left China. Our findings suggest that there is significant loss, but not as much as that suffered by Third World countries that lose fully trained faculty members, mostly because China to date has not produced many Ph.D.s. In our sample, only 9 people (3.3 percent) had already attained the Ph.D. before leaving China; the majority had completed their undergraduate training (49.1 percent) or had received an M.A. in China (44.6 percent) and had left China to get a Ph.D.[6] This situation reflects the "migration and education" pattern in Taiwan's and South Korea's brain drain, where students went to the United States to earn the Ph.D. but did not return. From this perspective, despite the fact that China does not produce a large number of undergraduate students and that the cost of training them is borne by the state, losing people with only a B.A. is more a loss of potential brainpower than a loss of already trained talent. On the other hand, if our sample is even somewhat representative of the Chinese student

---

[4] Xu Lin, lecture at Fairbank Center.

[5] Chang, "Causes of Brain Drain and Solutions," p. 42.

[6] We did not interview any undergraduates, believing that based on our definition, people who did not get any higher education in China do not represent a brain drain. Moreover, Orleans suggests that many people who came to the United States for undergraduate education as self-paying students probably were unable to get into Chinese universities. See Orleans, *Chinese Students in America*, p. 41.

population in the United States, then tens of thousands of very valuable M.A. students have been leaving China and not returning. For a society producing a limited number of Ph.D.s, the master's degree is quite important, as many of these people become university lecturers and form the key source of the future generation of Chinese scientists and researchers.[7] Moreover, as 45 percent of our sample (124) came to the United States to get Ph.D.s, the loss of potential brainpower is significant, especially if many of them do get this advanced degree and do not return to China.

To evaluate the significance of the loss we need to know what kind of people are leaning toward returning. Fortunately for China, our data show that people with B.A.s who came out to get M.A.s, and thus had lower educational levels (and perhaps lower educational aspirations), and in whom the Chinese government had made the least investment, are the least likely to return. Of this group, 42 percent tend toward staying. In contrast, visiting scholars, in whom the state has invested a great deal, are the most likely to return, with 59 percent leaning toward returning and only 15 percent leaning toward staying. Those who said that they came to the United States to get a Ph.D. also showed a significant desire to return. Of this group, 51 percent were leaning toward returning, while only 25 percent favored staying. Finally, 16.1 percent of our sample had received some research grant from the national, provincial, or municipal government or had done contract work for some Chinese enterprise—all of which signify a researcher of some quality. However, these people are much more likely to consider going home—10 of 43 (23.3 percent) are in category 1, while 17 of 43 (39.5 percent) are in categories 2 and 3.[8] These trends, then, show the brain drain to be less severe than many believed.[9]

---

[7] A full 33 percent of all M.A.s trained in 1985–90 by the Economic Training Center run by the Committee on Economic Education Research in China, funded by the Ford Foundation, had gone into university teaching with their M.A. degree. See Todd M. Johnson, "Program Evaluation Report: The Committee on Economic Education and Research in China," November 1991.

[8] The chi-square is significant at the .004 level. However, over 64 percent of these people do not have contact with their home unit more than once a year and are no more inclined than people who had not received grants in China to help either their colleagues or their unit back in China.

[9] Orleans argues that there are not enough good or appropriate positions for all the overseas Chinese Ph.D.s now being trained, so the fact that many do not want to return, he asserts, is not a disaster. Many available jobs are not in prestigious, coastal institutions, or they are in purely academic institutions, which cannot pay well. See Leo A. Orleans, "The Effects of China's 'Business Fever' on Higher Education at Home and on Chinese Students in the United States," *China Exchange News* 17.1 (March 1989): 11–13.

Evaluating the Brain Drain

Yet, regardless of their level of education when they left, many of these people are the cream of China's crop. Many gained access to the United States through very competitive exams, such as those employed by the Committee on Economics Education and Research in China (CEERC), funded by the Ford Foundation,[10] or based upon their Graduate Records Exam (GRE) and Test of English as a Foreign Language (TOEFL) scores. In the case of the China-U.S. Physics Examination and Application (CUSPEA) program, organized by T. D. Lee of Columbia University, the quality of the students who passed it, and thus were channeled into Ph.D. programs in the United States, was so high that many were offered jobs in the United States after graduation and have not returned. Second, even if China did not expend much money training these people, those who came to the United States on foreign funding used up very valuable international resources that otherwise could have gone to people who would return to work in China. For example, 25 percent of all M.A.s trained by CEERC went abroad for the Ph.D. If they do not return, the M.A. training they received from U.S. professors in China will have been of no benefit to China. The fact that all Ph.D.s trained in international affairs under the Committee on International Relations Studies with the PRC (CIRSPRC), a key Sino-American educational program funded by top U.S. foundations, did not return to China reflects an enormous loss in terms of "opportunity costs."[11] Similarly, that many of the people sent out to get Ph.D.s in the early- to mid-1980s under the World Bank loans have not returned to their universities has been a horrible loss for China.[12] Still, our data do show that those who

---

[10] The Ford Foundation, with the assistance of other foundations, funded three key programs in economics, international relations, and international law. These included the Committee on Economics Education and Research in China (CEERC), the Committee on International Relations Studies with the PRC (CIRSPRC), and the Committee on Legal Education Exchange with China (CLEEC). Their goals were to strengthen the teaching in these subjects at Chinese universities, and the programs often involved training graduate students and younger faculty both in China and in the United States. CLEEC also trained Chinese in legal research, not just teaching. See Johnson, "Program Evaluation Report," p. 35n.

[11] See Harry Harding, "An Evaluation of the Committee on International Relations Studies with the People's Republic of China and of International Studies in China" (unpublished report, June 23, 1992), p. 50. Overall the program had a 45 percent return rate, but the vast majority of the returnees were visiting scholars and participants in the mid-career M.A. program as compared to M.A. and Ph.D. candidates. The foundations included the Ford Foundation, the MacArthur Foundation, and the Luce Foundation. The Rockefeller Foundation and the Rockefeller Brothers Fund had been involved for several years but left the consortium in 1989.

[12] This finding is based on our interviews with World Bank Loan offices in seven universities in China in 1992. In each school, bank officials reported that very few, if any, of the people sent out to get Ph.D.s with World Bank funding had returned.

came to the United States on funds from international organizations lean toward returning more than those who did not.[13]

Aside from losing the potential resources, China now faces significant generational problems, particularly for its sciences, because of the brain drain. After the Anti-Rightist Campaign of 1957 and until the early 1980s, China trained no social scientists. Unless significant numbers of people trained abroad return, fields such as anthropology, sociology, and political science will have a hard time catching up to the West. Also, China has lost one generation of scientific researchers through the Cultural Revolution; these people, currently in their forties, did not receive proper scientific training in the 1960s and 1970s. Now the generation of people in their thirties, who were trained in the late 1970s and early 1980s and who might have picked up where the previous generation left off, is not returning. For example, one leading medical scientist we interviewed in 1992 at a medical university in southwest China, who had studied overseas twice, had applied to have his laboratory recognized as a National Research Laboratory. This status would have brought him significant national recognition and, more important, significant national funding. However, because his laboratory lacked any key researchers in their thirties, his application was denied. Having a successor generation in place is a necessary criterion for gaining this research status. Thus a 1988 survey of personnel at China's ten basic research institutes showed that 75.5 percent of China's researchers in the basic sciences are over forty years old.[14] The ramifications of this phenomenon for China's overall scientific development cannot be understated.

Thus there is the possibility of a real slowdown in scientific development on the Chinese mainland. Fortunately for China, more than 40,000 scholars who went overseas in the late 1970s and early 1980s returned, and today they are the core staff at the key research institutes and universities in China. Moreover, scholars who looked at China's science and technology system in the mid-1980s found that S&T research institutes in universities had undergone a major change under the reforms of the 1980s. Scientific and academic standards had greatly increased, and many important scientific findings had been made. Significantly, many of the people leading this revolution were returnees from overseas.[15] In

---

[13] The mean score on question 77 for people who came on funds from international organizations was 2.33; for those who did not come on international support, the mean score was 3.69; the population mean was 3.58. The probability of the chi-square was significant at the .004 level.

[14] See Kathlin Smith, "Red, Black, and Yellow Paths: New Choices for Young Scientists," *China Exchange News* 16.4 (December 1988): 14–15.

[15] See O. Schnepp, "The Impact of Returning Scholars on Chinese Science and Technology," in *Science and Technology in Post-Mao China,* ed. Denis Fred Simon and Merle

our own study, conducted in 1991–92, we found that compared to people who had not gone overseas, these returnees were better prepared for a global scientific revolution in at least ten major ways.[16] However, many of them had not been formally trained abroad but had gone overseas for only a year or two as visiting scholars. Had more of the people who had received systematic training in U.S. or foreign M.A. or Ph.D. programs or who had gained practical work experience returned, China's S&T system would have developed even more quickly.

Teaching programs in many institutions in China have suffered terribly from the brain drain and the fever to go abroad. Some departments that sent out their best students to gain Ph.D.s in the hopes that they would return to teach the next generation are at a standstill. One math department at a major institute in central China sent out twenty-two junior faculty to get Ph.D.s; none have returned. The large number of non-returnees increases the pressure on those in China to go overseas, as people become concerned that if they do not go out, others will assume they are not talented. So younger teachers who could fill the gap of the non-returnees are always looking for ways to go abroad.

What Benefits to China?

While most people we interviewed were unlikely to return in the near future, the overall loss would be lessened if these overseas scholars are contributing to China's modernization. Of the 273 people interviewed, only 22.3 percent were not helping their families in any way (or did not answer the question). The majority, 50.9 percent, were giving their families financial or material support of some kind, while another 18.7 percent were helping other family members get out of China. While the latter endeavor does not reflect well on China's future—indeed, suggests a continuing drain—the fact that over 50 percent of our sample were helping their families financially must be a positive sign from the government's perspective.

If people were helping their home unit, what form was that assistance taking? The limited frequency of interaction that most people had with their home unit challenges our hypothesis that the real cost of the brain drain was not so high because of the extensive contacts between people

---

Goldman (Cambridge: Harvard Contemporary China Series, 1989), pp. 175–98.

[16] See Chen and Zweig, "Impact of the Open Policy." Some of these characteristics include more efficient, more self-confident, and more creative work styles; better international contacts and research agendas; better facility with foreign languages, new technologies, and new research approaches; and greater financial security.

in the United States and their units back in China. Of the people who responded—there were 247 valid cases—37.7 percent had never had contact with their home unit or had no contact now, while 29.1 percent had contact only once a year (probably just a New Year's card from the unit as a way to maintain contact). Still, 23.1 percent had contact at least three times a year, and another 7.3 percent had contact six or more times a year. But because some in these two groups are planning to return immediately, we can only say that 24.7 percent of long-term sojourners have regular, extended contacts with their home unit.[17] While the contributions of this group might be important, fewer people than we anticipated had stable contacts with their home unit.

The types of interactions or exchanges vary. Of the 197 people who responded, 24 percent shared information about conditions in the United States, 21.4 percent exchanged research data, and 18.4 percent helped colleagues come to the United States as visiting scholars or students (this might include spouses). Among other forms of assistance, nine gave lectures, five gave financial support, five helped a delegation come over, and seventeen helped in some other way. Some people were involved in multiple forms of exchange, but at a minimum, by our calculations, 50.8 percent (100) of all people who responded to the question helped their unit in some way. From our perspective, the most positive finding is that 21.4 percent exchanged some research data, demonstrating that some intellectual transfer transpired. Also, some people may have helped units back in China other than their own.

We had expected to find more interaction between the students and scholars in the United States and their home units. In our research proposal we raised this as an important positive implication of the non-returnees staying in the United States. This was the position taken by the Chinese State Science and Technology Commission in September 1988, when it supported the idea of "storing brainpower overseas." We did find a significant correlation between a scholar's intention to return and the degree of contact with his or her home unit. In fact, the R^2 was .21. But this strong statistical relationship is also generated by the fact that people who have no contact do not plan to go back. On the other hand, because almost half our respondents had left China with a B.A. and as students may not have had close ties with any home unit, the fact

---

[17] Seven of the people who had contact with their unit six times a year or more were on their way home, while another 7 who were on their way home had contacts three times a year. If we subtract these 14 people, then 61 of 247 respondents (24.7 percent) interacted with their unit three times a year or more even though they were not on their way home immediately.

that 21.4 percent of respondents exchanged information is a positive sign. However, the fact that so many people do not have regular contacts with their home units, and that of those who do, a significant percentage is helping other people leave China, show that there are major limits to the flow of goods and services back to China by this group and that the type of information flows that are occurring—about how to get to the United States—also points to a continuing brain drain.

Why have these ties broken down? When asked, many people said that they had thought of maintaining ties with their original unit, but the chair of their department or their supervisor had changed, so when they contacted their unit again, no one responded. Others felt that after many years abroad, they had lost a common language. People in China, they felt, are not concerned about the problems of buying a house or raising children in the United States. Still others reported that they are afraid to have contacts with their home unit because they will be placed under enormous pressure to help their colleagues or their colleagues' children come out of China. In addition, they are constantly asked to host people in the United States who impose unfair burdens on them when they arrive. Also, people who are not planning to return do not want visitors or leaders from their original unit to find them after they come to the United States, so they do not give their addresses to those at home. Some people have strong reasons for cutting themselves off from their home unit, including abandoning a spouse in China or not wanting to repay their airfare to their home unit. In particular, those who promised to return or signed a contract with their home unit but who have since decided not to return consider cutting all ties to avoid any pressure from home once they get their spouse and family out.

Finally, with the dramatic increase in Sino-American economic ties, we hypothesized that some of these people would be helping to expand economic exchange. Of those among our sample who answered the question, 29 people (11.0 percent) were already involved in doing business with China, while 89 (37.2 percent) planned to do so.[18] Since many of the people we interviewed were students, we are not surprised that so few are involved in doing business with China. The key group, then, is

---

[18] Before Professor Chen went to Albuquerque, New Mexico, in September 1993, we had already completed 231 interviews in other cities and had done some analysis of those findings. Among that pre-Albuquerque group of 231 people, 27 (11.7 percent) were already doing business, and another 82 (35.5 percent) were planning to do so. That the percentages dropped significantly with the inclusion of the sample from Albuquerque suggests that if we looked primarily at places where opportunities and interests in doing business with China are greater—such as New York, Boston, or California—we would find a higher percentage of people interested in doing business.

those already out in the workforce. The fact that of the 77 people who are full-time employees only 16 people or 20.8 percent were doing business with China, while 3 of 17 part-time employees are doing business with China, suggests that in terms of direct business links with China, this group is not a major source of opportunity.

However, we carried out our interviews before the China business boom of 1993–94 had worked its way through the expatriate mainland Chinese community. The recent boom to do business with China has probably increased the number of Chinese in the United States doing business with China. And, if China's economy continues to grow at such a fast pace, if U.S. firms continue to invest in China, and if China avoids an economic crash as occurred in 1989–91, many of the Chinese students who received M.B.A.s in the United States in the past few years may get much more involved in the China trade.

How then do we assess the costs and benefits of the brain drain? Based on our analysis, we would suggest that the cup is either three-quarters empty or one quarter-full. In our previous work, we found that many people who went overseas in the early 1980s in the initial years of the exchange programs with the United States, Canada, Japan, Australasia, and Western Europe did return and have been making major contributions to China. But this group, which went abroad in its forties, is now in its fifties and needs a successor generation. Unfortunately, very few of the students and scholars currently in the United States, other than those who come as short-term visiting scholars, are likely to return in the near future to play that role.

There are some tiny silver threads in an overall bleak lining. First, China is not losing Ph.D.s in whom it has invested valuable resources. A significant number of Chinese students in the United States came out as undergraduates, and while there is a loss of potential brainpower, the real loss is less than the raw numbers of non-returnees would suggest. Second, significant numbers of people still interact with China, and over 20 percent of the exchanges involved research data of some type. Similarly, this group is beginning to play a role in promoting Sino-U.S. trade and in raising funds in the United States for investment in China.[19]

---

[19] The authors know two Chinese in the Boston area who went to Tufts University and are now raising funds in the United States for investment in China.

SEVEN

Bringing Them Home: Policy or Development?

There are several critical questions for the Chinese government and for international development agencies interested in training Chinese professionals and teachers who will work in China: Will more people return? How can one increase the return rate? Will more people return on their own initiative? Are there policies the Chinese government can initiate that will increase the return rate? What can donor agencies and the U.S. government do to ensure that more people trained overseas return? In this chapter we will address these and other related issues.

What percentage of the population of Chinese students and scholars are potential returnees? Of the 267 people who responded to question 77, other than people in category 1 (8.2 percent), who are already on their way home, people in categories 2 (24.7 percent) and 3 (19.9 percent), who comprise a total of 44.6 percent of our sample, are potential returnees, especially the 24.7 percent in category 2. This number is high, given the small numbers that actually are returning. Moreover, this desire by people in these two categories to stay linked with China and seriously to consider going home does not vary significantly whether they came before April 1990 (and are therefore eligible for the "June 4 green card") or after. This finding suggests that the desire to return among this population group is not conditioned by the difficulties or the ease encountered in staying. The question is how to bring them home.

Glaser proposed several strategies for bringing people home. First, he called for assertive "national leadership" to bring people home. Second, he agreed that although potential returnees would be attracted by higher pay, better facilities, more opportunities and assistance for research, and more international interaction, more than material rewards were needed: "professionals will stay in countries that have a sense of national purpose, where prospects seem bright for them and for their children, and where they feel wanted."[1] Glaser also found that although

---

[1] Glaser, *Brain Drain*, p. xiv.

few people were contacted by their governments or private employers after they had gone abroad, those who were contacted were more likely to return (but visits to the home country after studies were completed did not affect the numbers of people who were returning to live as compared to returning to visit). Also, informing students abroad about conditions at home and about new job opportunities were seen as important strategies. But most important, argued Glaser, governments must restructure domestic organizations and labor markets so people can change jobs more freely and feel that they can be promoted. These issues echo our perspective on the effect of the Chinese work unit on the brain drain and the problems that people face concerning job mobility back in China.

The successful efforts of South Korea and Taiwan to entice people to return, even after they have been abroad for many years, show that a proactive strategy by the home government can succeed. According to Yoon, Koreans have returned because of improved economic conditions, expanded employment opportunities, and widespread government action. In line with Glaser's recommendation, these people were made to feel wanted as the Korean government involved itself not only in the repatriation of scientists, but also in the "creation of a conducive environment which ranges from the creation of demands for repatriation to an ideological reorientation to protect professionalism."[2] The South Korean government built institutions for the newly returned scientists and offered them prestigious government jobs and research autonomy. Initially, repatriation expenses were borne by the state, and salaries were raised, although over time the private sector came to play a large role in funding repatriation. In short, Yoon argues that government programs redefined the role of returned scientists and engineers in Korean society and empowered them within the research institutes and the government, thereby creating a new "technocratic aristocracy."[3]

The government on Taiwan has also been active in enticing scientists and engineers to return. The Nationalist government has offered subsidies for travel, help in job placement, and assistance in business investment. On recruitment trips to the United States, government officials offered Taiwanese expatriates salaries competitive with U.S. incomes, improved working and living conditions, and school benefits.[4]

But what type of domestic political environment is necessary to attract people back? Must the home country become a democracy before

---

[2] Bang Soon Yoon, "Reverse Brain Drain in South Korea: State-Led Model," *Studies in Comparative International Development* 27.1 (Spring 1992): 8.

[3] Ibid., p. 17.

[4] Chang, "Causes of Brain Drain," pp. 38–42.

expatriates will return? Or is economic growth sufficient to draw people back? According to Huang, the correlation between the lack of political freedom in the home country and the student's decision to seek residency in the United States was so strong that for countries with poor human rights records, "simple appeals to patriotism and duty," even when accompanied by significant economic incentive packages, may be "futile unless matched by impressive progress in human rights conditions in the home country."[5] In the case of Taiwan, people did not return for almost two decades, and they did so only after the economy grew strong enough to offer significant financial rewards and excellent work conditions, and only after the political system liberalized. Not until people felt financially rewarded, politically secure, and intellectually free did the outward tide fall and the inward flow rise.

The Korean case, however, argues that even at lower levels of economic development, and even if the government remains authoritarian, a farsighted leadership that recognizes the critical role that foreign-trained scientists can play in creating a powerful research and development establishment can help bring people back. Korean efforts at reversing the brain drain began in the 1960s under Park Chung-hee, when Korea was poorer but looking to grow. The return flow continued right through the mid-1980s, during the time when Korea remained dominated by "bureaucratic authoritarianism." Overall, the number of returnees under these government-run programs is not large—only 1,707 had returned as of 1992 under permanent and temporary repatriation programs, while between 1953 and 1972, more than 10,400 Koreans petitioned the Ministry of Education for permission to study overseas.[6] Nevertheless, after the democratization of the late 1980s, the number of people seeking to return increased significantly, so that spaces are now unavailable, and the government has been forced to curtail its program.

China's government has begun to adopt similar proactive strategies. Recently, provincial officials from many coastal provinces, including Guangdong, Fujian, Jiangsu, Shandong, and Henan and from Shanghai and the Shenzhen Special Economic Zone traveled to the United States to try to attract scholars to return.[7] In these coastal localities, where provincial governments are richer and where income levels are increasing rapidly, people may find more enticing environments in which to live

---

[5] See Huang, "Empirical Analysis," p. 239.

[6] Yoon, "Reverse Brain Drain," p. 6.

[7] According to Kyna Rubin, more than fifteen such groups passed through Washington's Chinese embassy. See Kyna Rubin, "China Struggles to Turn the Tide of the Brain Drain," *Asian Wall Street Journal Weekly,* 17 January 1994.

and work. The Chinese government has also invited people back to visit and has instituted preferential housing policies for returned Ph.D.s. In addition, it has funded special programs to help returned Ph.D.s begin their research in China before they become established enough within the Chinese scientific and grant-earning community to be able to compete for grants. The government has also set up "Ph.D. stations" for those who return but cannot find an appropriate job. At these centers, returned scholars can carry out research and solve some of the problems they confront because they did not have a work unit when they left China. But national policies are often not implemented at the local level, either for lack of local funding or because of political factors within the home units to which these scholars return. Thus it is enormously important that the Chinese government follow through on its promises.

But what do our data say about the strategies proposed by Glaser? While Glaser does not believe that going back to visit increases people's willingness to return permanently, what do our data show? Recently, the Chinese government has called for scholars to come home and see how China has changed, but such visits may not always have a positive effect. One woman who visited China in the summer of 1993 for the first time in seven years found that people were too driven by the desire to earn money—the current national obsession—and bemoaned the loss of moral ties binding people together.

Our data support Glaser and suggest that visiting China has very little effect on one's view about returning. In our sample, 55 of 273 people had returned to visit. Of that group, 18 percent felt "very good" about their visit and 41.8 percent felt "good" about it. For the remaining 40 percent the trip generated feelings of ambivalence or had gone badly. However, of the 33 people who felt positive about the trip, 15 (45 percent) were in categories 2 and 3—leaning toward returning but having no plans. Such a trip may increase their chances of returning, despite the fact that for the population sample as a whole, there was no statistically significant relationship between how people felt about their visit and their views about returning.[8]

We asked people directly how their visit affected their views about returning, and again there was no significant relationship between these two factors. Moreover, only 2 of 49 who answered the question said

---

[8] However, for those who have a green card, the promise of the Chinese government that they will be allowed out again and the ability to return freely to the United States may combine to increase the number of Chinese from the United States who will visit China in the future. Reportedly, the number of visitors increased significantly in the summer of 1994.

that the trip "increased my desire to go back greatly." But of the 11 who said that the trip "greatly" or "somewhat" increased their desire to go back, 9 were in categories 2 and 3, and therefore may act upon those feelings. Going back increased the likelihood of *not* returning for only one person who was leaning toward returning, while for 11 of the 49 people who were leaning toward going back, it had no effect. Thus, inviting people to visit can only help: through such a trip Chinese scholars in the United States can establish new ties or revive dormant ties with units and people back in China; through these ties, commercial or scientific exchanges can develop. However, as far as people's views about returning are concerned, our data suggest that, in most cases, visits have little real effect.

Glaser also suggested that if home units have contact with people overseas, the probability of returning increases. Our data support this assertion, as there is a significant relationship between the frequency of contacts with the home unit and people's views about returning. Findings from our logistic regression are less consistent. Depending upon which variables are included in the model, significant readings can be found for the relationship between whether people think their unit wants them to return and what their plans are. However, in some cases it is a negative relationship.

Affording people the freedom to come and go is a major policy change. Will this policy, which is based on the hope that people were not returning because of fears of not being able to go out again, have any effect? According to our data, when asked why they themselves might choose not to return, of the 251 people who answered this question, only 6.4 percent of respondents chose either "difficulties getting out the first time" (3.2 percent) or "fears of not being able to get out a second time" (3.2 percent). Also, as one interviewee told us, units might allow people to go out a second time but charge them fees for leaving, especially if the unit realizes that the person is unlikely to return after the second trip out of the country. And even if charging fees does not prevent people from leaving, it certainly increases the costs of migration. Thus, although 82.6 percent of our interviewees knew about the policy change and nearly 65 percent of valid respondents to the question felt that this policy change was "very significant" (32.2 percent) or "somewhat significant" (32.2 percent), the policy may not affect many people's views about returning. Moreover, confidence about this policy is not high. Only 11.7 percent of our sample "completely" trust that the state will keep its promise, while another 39.3 percent trust it "somewhat" (see figure 8). Conversely, almost 50 percent of people do not trust the government or are uncertain that it will keep its promise. Still, even if this policy shift affects only 1–2 percent of the total mainland Chinese population in the United States, that means another 1,000 returnees.

Our findings also confirm the utility of many policy options raised by earlier studies. First, the percentage of older visiting scholars who return remains very high; therefore, increasing the numbers of older scholars, with established, stable roots in China, might increase the return rate. However, older visiting scholars may benefit less from a year abroad than younger scholars because of language limitations and the high start-up costs they incur in coming to America. As we looked around at the visiting scholar population, we were struck by the numbers of older visiting scholars who treat their year abroad as a vacation or as a reading opportunity. Little new research emerges from their visits to America.

Second, our findings show that once a scholar's spouse and child come out, the probability of returning drops precipitously. But limiting the opportunity for spouses to join their partners in the United States runs counter to human rights concepts of free migration and family reunification that are core to the American experience. However, officials in both the United States and China must recognize that allowing spouses out of China and into the United States greatly increases the brain drain.

Would major political changes in China bring more people back? Unlikely. First, major alterations to the nature of the regime would be accompanied by significant, and perhaps long-term, political unrest; as political instability is a major reason people do not return, such upheavals would probably increase the outflow and further decrease the number of returnees. And as only 12.4 percent of respondents in our sample chose political freedom as the main reason for not returning, a major political change in China without significant economic growth may not significantly affect the number of returnees. Increased economic opportunities, not political freedom, brought people back to Korea, which remained under an authoritarian regime. Because of the capricious nature of Chinese authoritarianism, however, Chinese citizens may be less willing than Koreans to adapt to continuing authoritarianism, and therefore political liberalism may be a prerequisite for more people to return.

Political considerations aside, because economic issues have an important effect on people's decision not to return, a large proportion of those interested in returning might do so if economic conditions were to improve. Therefore, the Chinese government's decision to promote greater reforms and rapid economic growth in China may be the best strategy for getting more people to return. As the controls of the work unit break down, as job mobility increases, and as returnees become able to work in units other than their original home unit, more people may return. An expanded foreign sector, which brings mainlanders back to China from overseas, could increase the return rate. However, bureaucratic allocations remain important for many jobs, while market forces, which would favor the interests of the returned scholars, are still in their developmental stage. Therefore, a very activist government strategy, initiated by central leaders or by a powerful ministry, is necessary to reverse the brain drain. The role of Park Chung-hee in Korea shows that strong central leadership that favors people who return is necessary to overcome vested interests within the country. President Park gave returned scholars important social status, something that this leadership in China is reluctant to do. Although statements such as those by Party General Secretary Jiang Zemin, where he denied that returnees needed to demonstrate a "communist concept of life," asking instead only for patriotism because "a son will not mind his mother's being ugly," are helpful,[9] Chinese leaders still see returnees as a political threat, carrying the virus of "bourgeois liberalization." The mistrust these overseas scholars feel puts them in a different situation from returnees to Korea and Taiwan and makes them less willing to return.

Yet the Chinese government is in a quandary. To bring people back from overseas it must offer returnees handsome rewards—better housing, higher salaries, and preferred jobs. But doing so skews the incentive structures for those still in China who are seeking to advance their own careers by showing them that the route to higher salaries, good housing, and top jobs passes through Ph.D. programs at foreign universities. Then, once people go overseas and taste the freedom, salaries, housing, and stability of Western life, the problem of the brain drain emerges. Thus it is not surprising to find that the Chinese government offers these special privileges only grudgingly.

But even grudgingly given special privileges are difficult to come by. When implementation of national policies is left to individual units or local communities, the jealousy of those who have not been overseas or who did not get advanced degrees toward those who have been overseas and resentment at giving them special privileges limit the capability of individual units to improve the work conditions of the returnees. In one university in central China, for instance, the faculty voted down the idea of building a special "Ph.D. building" (*bo shi lou*) for returnees. Also, funds within most research and educational units are insufficient to generate strong economic incentives to return.[10] As personal links between

---

[9] See *People's Daily,* 14 March 1990, p. 1.

[10] The one trained Ph.D. in a science and technology university in Chengdu was an unmarried only son who returned because his parents needed his help.

directors of research institutes and faculty overseas wane, personal relations do not push institute directors to bring people back. The task requires strong national leadership, but the central government and the SEDC are too cash poor to introduce the type of central government policies that worked in Korea. Even if the central government expanded the number of posts at research institutes under the Chinese Academy of Sciences, new positions as a percentage of the outflow would be minuscule. Moreover, the academy's recent policy is to cut the number of positions significantly. Perhaps as wealthier provincial governments or large industrial conglomerates try to expand their own research and development capacities, they will fulfill the role played by the private sector in Korea. Similarly, new high-tech industrial parks may offer good housing and high salaries to attract people back, but many of these parks are either under pressure to provide housing for university faculty affiliated with the parks or are in out-of-the-way sites to which few locals, never mind people overseas, would want to move.

Because of a shortage of funds, the Chinese government has resorted to its familiar and comfortable method of propaganda. Through several newspapers, including the Overseas Edition (*haiwai ban*) of the *People's Daily* and the *Guangming Daily,* which are often read by students and scholars overseas, the Chinese government has tried to affect the decisions of Chinese scholars about whether to go abroad, where they should go, and whether they should come home. A series of articles in the *Guangming Daily* in 1991–92 summarized the backgrounds of returnees and portrayed their lives in China in a very positive light.[11] Also, a series of letters in the Overseas Edition of the *People's Daily* told of promotions, funding support, and other aspects of what Broaded called an "ideal absorption" process.[12] Another series of letters in this paper painted a bleak picture of life in the United States for Chinese sojourners, comparing the cold reception they received from Americans to the response of Japanese people, who are seen as being much more hospitable to Chinese students and scholars.[13] Because Japan is much less flexible in allowing Chinese to overstay their visas, the return rate

---

[11] A series of approximately fifty articles, entitled "'Liu xue gui lai' you jiang zheng wen" (A series of solicited articles about the accomplishments of 'returned students'), was published from September through December 1991 in the *Guangming ribao* (Guangming daily), the key newspaper for Chinese intellectuals. The series was coordinated by the Department of Returned Students in the State Education Commission.

[12] For an evaluation of these letters and an analysis of China's strategy, see C. Montgomery Broaded, "China's Response to the Brain Drain," *Comparative Education Review* 37.3 (August 1993): 277–303.

[13] Ibid.

from Japan is higher than from the United States. These articles thus reflect China's strategy to increase return rates by channeling fewer people to the United States. Aware that it is propaganda, most overseas students and scholars in the United States do not put much stock in such reports. However, the articles may have some effect on older scholars, people who are leaning toward returning, or people with strong ties on the mainland—categories 2 and 3.

Finally, what role should the U.S. government and international donors play in getting Chinese to return?[14] The U.S. government should follow its present path: push for gradual, but continuing, reform of China's polity and economy, but recognize that if the goal is to get people to return to China, a rapid transition to democracy is likely to be highly destabilizing in a political system that has little democratic tradition or experience and no organized, institutionalized opposition to assert control during a period of transition. While a more democratic China may in the long run be more stable (and would clearly be preferable to the increasingly corrupt regime that is emerging), the transition from hard authoritarianism to democracy in a country of one billion people can be enormously risky for all Chinese citizens. Unless their goal in returning is to participate directly in the politics or economics of transition, rather than simply to find a good, stable job and raise their family, the vast majority of Chinese in the United States will see life in America as enormously more secure than life in a China undergoing rapid socioeconomic and political transformations.

Given the nonpolitical concerns of these sojourners—for better economic conditions, greater job mobility, and better housing—a greater economic engagement by the U.S. government and the U.S. business community may increase the number of returnees. Higher-paying jobs in the foreign sector can serve as a drawing card. As the United States presses China to protect copyrights and patents and to liberalize its domestic labor laws, the work environment for Chinese scientists and researchers may improve. They will be better positioned to reap economic profits from the knowledge and innovations they bring back from overseas. On the other hand, an improved intellectual property rights regime may prevent many returnees from making money by marketing foreign products or using foreign patents within China illegally. Still, as more and more Chinese develop a personal stake in maintaining an open policy to the outside world, prospective returnees may feel more

---

[14] The following are the views of Professor Zweig, but not necessarily those of Professor Chen.

secure about their ability to make future trips abroad or maintain stronger links with the global scientific community after they return.

Current efforts by aid agencies, such as the Ford Foundation's decision to fund the China Economic Research Center for returnees at Beijing University, may be an important new direction in helping people return. Foundations are particularly interested in seeing people they have trained return to China, and our data show that people who were funded by international organizations are more inclined toward returning than the rest of the sample.[15] Creating "small environments" of reform (what some reformers called *xiao huanjing*) has been a successful strategy in the past, in that people outside that environment begin to demand equal opportunities for themselves. The reforms, therefore, can spread. Especially if the Chinese government turns to returned economists, accepts some of their research findings, and heeds some of their policy advice, more scholars in the social sciences will be interested in returning. Such centers were key to bringing scholars back to South Korea, and in today's Taiwan many people in key government think tanks are returned Ph.D.s.

However, advisers who remained in China after Tiananmen and who have reemerged as policy advisers following several years in political oblivion will hardly welcome these "outsiders" with equanimity. Similarly, many political bureaucrats will still mistrust these "foreign" ideas. Should these "small environments" remain isolated pockets of returnees, with little influence, the experiment may prove less successful; therefore, serious efforts must ensue to incorporate these people into policy research. Moreover, the favorable conditions this limited number of returnees will receive will reinforce the current perception that the road to academic success or status passes through the visa section at U.S. consulates in China. In this way, these centers may become just one more incentive for the best and the brightest to leave the country, thereby contributing to the outward flow without greatly influencing the number of people who ultimately return.

There are no easy answers to reversing the brain drain. Experimentation is necessary and to be applauded. The United States must be patient with the slow pace of change, especially regarding political reforms, in

---

[15] Of the 21 people we interviewed who were financed by international donors, such as the Ford Foundation, United Nations Development Program, World Health Organization, Fulbright, and the like, 7 had plans to return, 8 were in category 2, and 1 was in category 3. There was a significant relationship (the probability of the chi-square was significant at the .004 level) between being funded by an international donor and one's views about going back.

China. While a stable and economically developed China is needed to bring people home, one must recognize that rapid economic growth is itself inherently unstable; moreover, it is highly unlikely that prosperity, stability, and liberty will all occur in the short run.

Conclusion

When China's leaders decided to expand educational exchanges to draw in technological benefits from the West, they did not anticipate the brain drain that has ensued. Deng Xiaoping reportedly argued that even if China *lost* 5 percent of its scholars to the West, the open policy in education would still be a success. Given that little more than 5 percent are currently returning, it is little wonder that so much soul searching has been going on in Beijing and that policy on sending students abroad has gone through numerous permutations. Clearly, the leadership never anticipated this "fever to go abroad" (*chu guo ri*) or that so few people would want to return.[1] It felt that patriotism would keep people attached to their homeland. But the economic gap between East and West, the political instability in China in the late 1980s, the continuing concerns about the post-Deng transition, and the desires of talented people for an environment in which they can develop and use their skills have all come together to generate China's brain drain.

In many ways, the sources of China's brain drain do not differ significantly from those that have affected other developing countries. We have seen this in the case of Taiwan, which also suffered very low return rates until the 1980s. Lakshmana Rao, in his 1978 study, cited four key factors pulling people from developing to advanced countries: salary, logistical support, political stability, and opportunities for mobility. While few people (5.6 percent) in our study chose logistical support as an important reason, our findings show that Chinese students and scholars in the United States share many of these other concerns and hopes. No doubt, had the June 4 Tiananmen incident not taken place, triggering a U.S. government policy that greatly simplified remaining in the United States, more Chinese might have returned. This type of politically generated brain drain is not very common, although many Iranians stayed in the United States after the fall of the shah in 1979. But the trend against returning among Chinese in the United States had emerged

---

[1] See Xiao Qinfu, "Di si ci lang chao: Chu guo ri" (The fourth wave: The fever of going abroad), in *Wuce lang chao* (The five waves), ed. Xiao Qinfu et al. (Beijing: People's University Press, 1989), pp. 138–90.

strongly by 1987; Tiananmen solidified that trend and made it easier to stay.

A multitude of complex factors affects people's reasons for returning or staying. While we do not want simply to restate our key findings here, several points should be emphasized. The sex of the respondent and family ties, particularly the transition from being a single student to a married adult with children, greatly affect perceptions about returning. While this transition may not affect the probability of returning, it does change the reasons for people's decisions. Song's study of Koreans in the United States cited previously also shows that people with families in the United States respond quite differently from those without.[2] Having children weakens political concerns and raises the importance of housing and perhaps concerns about the children's future. And because China treats women and men differently, women's views about returning differ from men's. In fact, more women than men never planned to go back in the first place.

As to whether politics or economics is driving this brain drain, both factors are at work. But because people's political concerns focus more on issues of stability than on abstract concerns of political freedom, and because many also care about economic factors, we anticipate that China will follow the pattern of Taiwan and Korea. Compared to studies done a few years ago, our data suggest that the effect of Tiananmen has decreased. As economic and social conditions liberalize and improve, if China's government becomes more proactive in recruiting and if the post-Deng era proves to be relatively stable, Chinese students and scholars will return to their homeland in larger numbers than today. But the continuing pull of high salaries, better housing, overall better living conditions, and easier job mobility will keep the vast majority of Chinese in the United States. Moreover, given the high percentage of Chinese J-1 visa holders who successfully switched to other visa statuses, and who continue to do so, the brain drain to the United States will continue, even among visiting scholars.

Government policy on the open door in education contributes to China's brain drain in several ways that differ from the effect in most other developing states. Leadership fears in Beijing about the continuing brain drain and sporadic government efforts to control it simply fuel the fever to go abroad. Because so many policies in China are unstable, people race forward in enormous numbers when opportunities first appear, terrified that if they miss the train at the first station, the chance to board will be gone forever. Policies regarding overseas education

---

[2] See Song, "Who Stays? Who Returns?"

have been as unstable as any others in China, so every time a policy is liberalized, people rush to take advantage of it. This has been especially noticeable since the mid-1980s. Also, because China has not invested enough funds in improving the work and living environments for intellectuals in China, and because returnees find a cultural and political climate that questions their loyalty, the people who go out do not want to return. In this situation we are observing a brain drain "with Chinese characteristics."

But the low return rates are not an unmitigated evil for China, except perhaps to a leadership that sees any signs of disloyalty as direct challenges to its legitimacy. Many of the people China is losing are following the "migration then education" patterns: they are not being trained in China and then leaving, but are being trained abroad at the expense of the host country, in this case the United States and U.S. academic institutions. Therefore, the real, as compared to opportunity, costs to the Chinese state are not very high (while the foreign country paying for the graduate training of a multitude of Chinese is reaping some benefits of that investment). Should more Chinese students and scholars return in the long term, China will benefit from funds and human capital expended by U.S. academics and institutions. Second, as in Korea, where there is intense competition for good academic jobs, many of the Chinese sojourners, even if they chose to return now, might not find appropriate or satisfying jobs in China today. Dissatisfied with their conditions, they could become a further source of political and social instability.

Despite low return rates, a significant cohort has not closed off the possibility of returning. If our sample is at all representative, there are about 10,000 students and scholars who, in both the short and long run, are still considering returning to the mainland. And if even a small percentage of these people do eventually return, bringing with them the very skills, technology, and capital that motivated the initial opening to the outside world in 1978, it will be of enormous benefit to China. Moreover, given the current level of trans-Pacific interactions, China continues to benefit significantly from its open policy in education, and over time, as more and more Chinese take up important positions in the United States and as China undergoes further reforms, this group of scholars will help expand U.S.-China ties and help promote economic, educational, and political development on the China mainland.

Methodological Issues in Choosing Our Sample

We wanted to choose a representative sample that would allow us to generalize across the entire population of Chinese students and scholars in the United States. We knew that many researchers had been sending out questionnaires to Chinese scholars in the United States, but we had concerns about that method. While one gets more responses at lower costs, asking many detailed questions greatly reduces the response rate. Also, while response rates to surveys in the early post-Tiananmen period had been relatively high—Huisong Yuan got a 50 percent response rate for his 1989–90 survey of Chinese students in Canada—we were warned that as of 1992–93, Chinese students and scholars had lost interest in facilitating such studies and were now even less likely to respond. If our response rate was under 30 percent, we could not assert with confidence that we had anything near a population from which to generalize.[1] Also, because we were doing the study only shortly before the July 1, 1993, opening day to apply for permanent resident status under the Chinese Students Protection Act, we feared that ever-cautious Chinese students and scholars would be even more unlikely to respond to an unsolicited mailed questionnaire. Finally, because of the Ford Foundation's generous support we had the funds to bring Professor Chen over from China for ten months to carry out the interviews.

Therefore, we chose to use a face-to-face interview format, employing a research instrument of 105 questions. Through direct interviews we could get more information than would be available from an impersonal questionnaire. Professor Chen, who did most of the interviews, could meet people in their homes, see how they lived, and, we hoped,

---

[1] Parris Chang and Zhiduan Deng got a response rate of only 32.5 percent from a mailed survey in 1989. See Chang and Deng, "The Chinese Brain Drain and Policy Options." We felt that this response rate allowed for a large, undecipherable bias among both those who chose to respond and those who refused to respond.

get them to talk in greater depth about their views and hopes about going home and staying in America.

Where our work differs most from other studies is that we interviewed more than just students. Two other groups needed to be studied: visiting scholars, who are most likely to return, and people who had already graduated and were out in the workforce. Therefore, although we interviewed many graduate students (we felt that undergraduate students in the United States, who had not gone to a university in China, did not constitute a brain drain), we added visiting scholars and people in the workforce to our interview population.

We pretested our questionnaire in Toronto in fall 1992. The main revision we made based on that pretest was to alter the dependent variable, question 77, about people's views about returning. In Toronto, we used a five-point scale, asking people only about their attitudes about returning. But when 25 percent of the interviewees said that they would "definitely return," we revised the question. The fact that Professor Chen had interviewed a large number of visiting scholars who had come after 1991 partly explained these findings. Most of these people had to go back. But our concern was to differentiate between those who "said" they were definitely going back and those who in fact were already "planning" to go back. So we divided those who were "definitely returning" into two categories: those who were "definitely going back and have plans" and those who were "definitely going back but have no plans." We also differentiated among those who said they were "probably" going back by dividing this group into those "with good ties to China" and those "without strong ties." Our assumption is that those who said they "probably" would go back but did not have strong ties in China were unlikely to return but unwilling to say so. We also chose to decrease the number of visiting scholars within our sample, as they were more likely to return than were other groups.

Despite our decision to employ interviews rather than a mailed questionnaire, we still found that many people refused to talk with us. Some refused to cooperate when they heard that the questionnaire took more than an hour to administer. Others played it safe and refused to talk with us because the July 1 deadline for applying for permanent residence status was approaching.

To decrease the refusal rate, and because many people expressed concerns about the politically sensitive nature of this topic, we asked fewer political questions. Yet through more indirect means we found ways for people to express their political concerns, and many more did so than we had anticipated. As a result, we were able to build two political indicators that demonstrated a statistically significant relationship with people's decisions about returning. This finding makes us feel relatively confident about our sample and our survey instrument.

To achieve as random and representative a population as possible, we adopted the following strategy. First, we chose different types of people—scholars, students, and people in the workforce. Second, we surveyed several regions in the United States and several communities, with varying densities of Chinese students and scholars. This way we could see what life was like for students in the more cosmopolitan, as compared to more isolated, U.S. communities. Thus we chose schools in the Northeast, the Southwest, and upper New York state and on the West Coast.

To achieve randomness, we chose our informants randomly from lists of students drawn up in advance. To get such lists we had to contact schools that had such lists and would share them with us. Not all Chinese student organizations were willing to share their membership rosters with us. Thus we spent a great deal of time contacting Chinese student associations on various campuses in Boston and California. Because of some resistance to share these lists, we also went to both the State University of New York in Buffalo and the University of New Mexico in Albuquerque, which have relatively large student populations and where we had contacts among the Chinese student groups.

In certain instances we could not get lists of all Chinese graduate students because the directors of the universities' international centers felt strongly that supplying this information conflicted with people's rights to privacy, so we built them ourselves. At Harvard, we used a graduate student telephone directory. Unfortunately, this strategy creates a bias toward those who have offices on campus, who are probably also more stable and successful than students who have no office. Even so, we were not always successful in getting lists of names. For Tufts University, we had to contact the graduate colleges on campus directly and build our own list.[2] In Buffalo, our Chinese contacts were not well

---

[2] The Tufts University Chinese Student Association said it needed to call a meeting of all its members before it could authorize giving us a list. Because we feared that a negative response would cause the Chinese students to hesitate to talk with us, we decided not to ask them to call such a meeting and therefore never sought their approval. Also, the director of Tufts University's International Students Office felt that for reasons of privacy, she could not in good conscience give us a list. In the end, we built our own list by going through the lists of graduate students from various graduate programs. We then chose those students who had used the mainland romanization system, called *pinyin*, as we assumed that they were from the mainland. Hong Kong Chinese, as well as students from Taiwan or Singapore, were likely to use another romanization system. Nevertheless, any mainland student who used a different romanization system was unfortunately excluded by this method from our larger population.

connected on campus, so, while we got a complete list more readily, the rejection rate was higher. We also wanted to get students from different kinds of schools. In the Boston area we interviewed students at Harvard, Tufts, and Boston University. We had hoped to interview students at Northeastern University, which has a co-op program, but we were unable to build bridges with the Chinese student groups there. Nevertheless, interviews at SUNY-Buffalo and the University of New Mexico gave us a chance to talk to Chinese students who were enrolled in less prestigious schools in the United States.

Using only those people who could be contacted (lists were sometimes out of date or lacking key information), we built our list of students. We felt strongly, and many people reinforced this view, that a person's area of study would be an important factor determining his or her view about returning.[3] Therefore, we classified all interviewees into six academic fields: natural sciences; applied natural sciences; business, foreign trade, and management sciences; applied social sciences (economics, law);[4] social sciences; and humanities and the arts. The percentage in each academic field in our sample was determined by the percentage of Chinese students at that campus enrolled in that field. For example, in Buffalo, the Chinese Students and Scholars Association gave us a list of 500 people. After trying to contact all these students, we found that 277 people were still at the same telephone number. Using this list, we calculated the percentage of Chinese students in each academic field.

Based on these percentages, we decided on the number of students to be interviewed from each academic field. After we composed the list in alphabetical order in each field,[5] we then divided the number of students in the population by the number of people to be sampled for the field, which then determined the frequency with which we would choose a name from the list. Thus, for example, if there were 107 natural sciences students, and we needed to interview eight people, we divided 107 by 8 and chose every thirteenth person on the list. If the percentage of students in some fields was too small, we increased the number of people that were chosen from that field.

---

[3] As it turned out, we found only a limited relationship between a student's or scholar's field of study and her or his views about returning.

[4] The idea here is that people in these fields could more easily apply their skills to finding jobs in the U.S. work place, while those in the purer social sciences would have greater difficulty. We had originally put education in the "applied" category, but based on suggestions by specialists in international education, we placed it in the humanities field.

[5] In Chinese, placing the names in alphabetical order in no way affected the selection process, as there is nothing that would affect the random nature of an alphabetical list.

We followed a similar strategy to choose our population of people who had graduated and were already out working. In each city we compiled a list of people by asking friends, and friends of friends, to recommend people who might be interviewed. We were always careful to get these lists from different types of Chinese, including those involved in politics, business, and educational research. Again, we compiled a list of names in alphabetical order and chose from the list based on the total number of people we hoped to interview. For example, in New York, we built a list of 91 people. Because 25 people were to be interviewed, we chose every fourth name on the list (91/25=4).

Because the number of visiting scholars is small and changes yearly, it was not easy to get a complete list of names. Therefore, we did not choose the visiting scholars randomly but only ensured representation from different academic fields, different age groups, both sexes, and different lengths of time in the United States. Still, we hoped that those who were chosen would be representative of the total population of visiting scholars.

When making the appointments and doing the actual interviews, we had two concerns: whether people would agree to be interviewed and whether they would answer honestly. These concerns conflicted with our desire for randomness, in that people chosen completely at random might be less forthcoming. Although we selected people at random from lists, to solve the problem of "responsiveness" we hired a student in each city to make the contacts and arrangements. Whenever possible, we chose people to make contacts for us who had lived in the locality for some time, had extensive contacts with Chinese students in the city, had some standing in the Chinese student community, understood survey methodology, and would strictly follow these research methods. They informed prospective informants about our project, including the content, purpose, and methods of the study, our desire to publish the final output, and the background of the researchers. In many instances, our Chinese contacts actually knew the people we interviewed. Professor Chen also volunteered information about our study during the actual interview. As an inducement, and to show our appreciation for their cooperation, we offered each person we interviewed $10.

Our rate of refusal varied in part according to the person who was making the contacts for us. Where we were able to use the personal ties of Chinese students who were leaders in a local student organization, we had a lower refusal rate. Thus in Albuquerque, the refusal rate was only about 10 percent.[6] On the other hand, the Buffalo refusal rate was over

---

[6] In Albuquerque, the person making contacts for us said that only 5 people out of 52 refused to be interviewed. More had initially refused, but he persuaded them that their

30 percent because the facilitator had been there only three years and had not participated in many student activities. He knew few of the people he contacted. In Boston, the refusal rate varied from school to school. Our contact person had graduated from Tufts and was getting his Ph.D. at Harvard, so the refusal rate at those places was low. But when he approached students at Boston University the refusal rate increased to about one-third. In New York, the refusal rate was over 50–60 percent because the people we interviewed were almost all in the workforce and were often holding two jobs. Moreover, our contact knew very few of them.

While our overall rejection rate was comparatively low, we did wonder why almost one-third of the people refused to talk with us. People justified their refusal to meet with us in four ways. First, people were busy; many students we approached in April suggested waiting until after exams. Unfortunately, we could not wait. Second, some people wanted us to mail the questionnaire to them so they could study it first and then decide if they wanted to be interviewed. These people were concerned about possible political complications. We did not comply with their requests, but simply skipped them and moved on to the next name on the list. Third, some said that they could not bear to look back on unpleasant events from the past, such as how their families had suffered during the 1950s or the Cultural Revolution.[7] Finally, some claimed that they had been too deeply involved in the Tiananmen events (either in China or in the United States) and were unwilling to have any contact with strangers from China. Many of these people did not believe that this was a scholarly study; they were worried that we were sent by either the Chinese or the U.S. government. They feared that our study was related to the pending decision on permanent residence status. Some feared that publication of the research might cause them trouble. Nevertheless, except for our interviews in New York, our refusal rate was much lower than that for most mailed surveys; thus, the sample is more reliable.

The willingness to be interviewed also varied across the different groups of people. Visiting scholars were most agreeable to be interviewed, currently enrolled students less so, while those who were employed were the most difficult to interview. Those in the natural sciences were more willing to be interviewed than people in the social

---

fears about future problems and about the political background of the interviewer were unfounded.

[7] Since so many people were intellectuals or children of intellectuals, most had had very difficult experiences during these two periods.

sciences, who were more political and more suspicious. Those already holding green cards and those who were ineligible for protection under the Chinese Students Protection Act had fewer worries than those who were waiting to get a green card. Geographically, those in more remote cities, like Buffalo and Albuquerque, were more easygoing and less suspicious than those in big cities.

One issue we were unable to assess was the effect that the ethnicity of the interviewer may have had on our responses. Some people, especially non-Chinese, assert that Chinese speak more openly to non-Chinese, feeling that political repercussions are less likely if the interviewer is not Chinese. On the other hand, if the interviewer is a Caucasian, his or her power and status in the United States might affect how the interviewee answers the questions. Most of our interviews were carried out by Professor Chen, a mainland scholar who edits an educational journal with some ties to the State Education Commission. For this reason, some of the interviewees might have been cautious in talking with him. The approximately 80 interviews in California were carried out by two graduate students from the University of Southern California, one a woman from China, the other, a white male. However, while we would have liked to evaluate the effect of the interviewer on the responses, we had no way to do so, as Professor Chen did too many of the interviews to allow us to analyze this variable. Still, because Professor Chen did most of the interviews, any bias that emerged would be relatively consistent.

In the end, we believe that people who agreed to be interviewed generally revealed their actual situation and true thoughts. Because many of our questions related to specific problems people faced in their work, their studies, and their lives both before they left China and since their arrival in the United States, it was less necessary for them to distort their answers. Also, that so many people told us that they never had planned to return makes us feel that they answered truthfully on most questions. But we do have some doubts about the answers to our dependent variable, question 77. We believe that those who said that they would "probably return but did not know when" are unlikely to return; so we treated these people as if they would not return and moved their response on our scale of views about returning from the fourth position to the fifth position, on the other side of those who were uncertain. Also, it is possible that people shied away from quickly admitting that their main purpose in staying was economic; but as outlined above, we used several strategies to adjust for that issue. Otherwise we believe that people were relatively open about their feelings about returning. As for people who told involved stories about their lives in China or the United States, we often tried to verify these stories from third parties. In general, the information people provided and the thoughts they expressed seemed credible.

Our Application of Multivariate Logistic Regression Analysis

Standard regression analysis assumes that the variables being analyzed are interval-level data, that is, that the data run on a continuum (such as from low to high) and that the distance between each category or step in the variable is the same. Our key dependent variable, people's attitudes about returning, may not fit that bill. When we composed the question to tap people's views about returning, we anticipated doing standard regression analysis. Hence we structured question 77 to reflect a clear progression from "definitely going back and have already made plans," through "unsure" as the mid-point, to "definitely not returning." To make it more linear, we moved the category "probably will return but do not have strong ties to China" from the fourth position in the progression to the fifth, on the other side of those who were uncertain about returning, to make the data read more like interval data. Also, when we did the interviews, we offered the choice of "uncertain" at the end, rather than in the middle of this progression; but when we did our analysis, we put it in the middle. Nevertheless, our categories, while reflecting the properties of interval data, are in reality based on different categories of people's views about returning.

To ensure that our analysis had statistical merit, we used a form of multiple regression called logistic regression analysis. Although this form of analysis does not allow us to measure the relative effects of the different independent variables on our dependent variable, because there is no correlation coefficient, it does allow us to use a multivariate analysis methodology without having to assume that categorical data are actually interval-level data. Also, the relative values of the parameter estimates suggest which independent variables are more or less important.

The most important result, however, is the probability chi-square that we received for each variable. This score tells us whether or not the variables included in our regression model have a significant effect on our outcome variable, the decision to return to China or stay in the United States, when all the variables in the model are included in the analysis. Thus we can feel very confident that any variable for which the probability of the chi-square is less than .05 does affect the decision about returning or staying. We may also assume a relatively strong relationship exists between the independent and dependent variables even when the probability of the chi-square is less than 0.1.

Structuring and Analyzing our Dependent Variable

In our bivariate analysis (analysis between two variables), when we wanted to see the strength of the relationship between one variable and people's views about returning, we sometimes treated the responses to question 77 as interval data running from 1 through 7. We did this particularly when we wanted to see the correlation coefficient or the R^2 in a regression. However, in most cases, when we used a chi-square test, we were treating question 77 as categorical data. Similarly, when we used the responses in our logistic analysis, we structured the responses to question 77 in different ways. The following two ways seemed most appropriate: First, and what we refer to as "version 1," was to use the data in its natural form, as categorical data running from 1 through 7. To do this we had already moved the "unsure" response from the seventh category, where it was in the questionnaire, to the fourth or middle point, shifting the fourth response, "probably will go back but have not kept up ties," to fifth position and the fifth and sixth choices into the sixth and seventh positions.

Version 2 involved restructuring the response variable, collapsing the "definitely going back" categories (1: "definitely going back and have made arrangements to do so" and 2: "definitely going back but don't know when") into one category. Our second category in this progression was those who were less certain about going back, including those in category 3, who said that they "probably will go back and have kept up strong ties," those in (new) category 4, who said that they "can't really say now," and those in (new) category 5, who said that they "probably will go back but have not kept up ties." We combined these three responses into our second category. Our last category combined old category 5 (new 6), where people chose "not very likely to go back, but might do so if things changed in China greatly," and category 6 (new 7), where people chose "definitely will not go back."

We grouped the response variable into three larger categories for reasons of statistical efficiency. Because the number of cases—273—is relatively small, and we had 15 independent variables whose effect on the dependent variable had to be measured, we could increase the quality of the analysis by collapsing our dependent variable into three, rather than seven, categories. Both versions of our dependent variable generated some significant statistical relationships, although version 2, because it was more efficient, tended to give us better readings. We chose to report the results of both versions, as they both reflect the responses we received; they just structure those responses in different ways.

Finally, we also chose to rerun the logistic regression analysis one last time without including the choices about the children's education to see if and how the scores would change. We did this in part because the scores for question 55 and question 56, plans for children's education, in our logistic regression were not significant. Thus the chi-square scores differ in tables 8 and 9 because those two variables have been removed from the model in table 9. In most cases, more scores in table 9 are statistically significant, suggesting that this is a more representative model of the key determinants of people's decisions about not returning. Also, no variables that were significant in table 8 disappear in table 9, while some that were not significant in table 8 are now significant in table 9.

President Bush's Executive Order, April 11, 1990

Executive Order 12711 of April 11, 1990
The President: Policy Implementation with Respect to Nationals of the People's Republic of China

By the authority vested in me as President by the Constitution and laws of the United States of America, the Attorney General and the Secretary of State are hereby ordered to exercise their authority, including that under the Immigration and Nationality Act (a U.S.C. 1101-1887), as follows:

Section 1. The Attorney General is directed to take any steps necessary to defer until January 1, 1994, the enforced departure of all nationals of the People's Republic of China (PRC) and their dependents who were in the United States on or after June 3, 1989, up to and including the date of this order (hereinafter "such PRC national").

Section 2. The Secretary of State and the Attorney General are directed to take all steps necessary with respect to such PRC nationals (a) to waive through January 1, 1994, the requirement of a valid passport and (b) to process and provide necessary documents, both within the United States and at U.S. consulates overseas, to facilitate travel across the borders of other nations and reentry into the United States in the same status such PRC nationals had upon departure.

Section 3. The Secretary of State and the Attorney General are directed to provide the following protections:

SOURCE: *Interpreter Releases: Report and Analysis of Immigration and Nationality Law* 67.15 (April 16, 1990): 447–48.

(a)

irrevocable waiver of the two-year home country residence require-ment that may be exercised until January 1, 1994, for such PRC nationals;

(b)

maintenance of lawful status for purposes of adjustment of status or change of nonimmigrant status for such PRC nationals who were in lawful status at any time on or after June 3, 1989, up to and includ-ing the date of this order;

(c)

authorization for employment of such PRC nationals through January 1, 1994; and

(d)

notice of expiration of nonimmigrant status (if applicable) rather than the institution of deportation proceedings, and explanation of options available for such PRC nationals eligible for deferral of enforced departure whose nonimmigrant status has expired.

Section 4. The Secretary of State and the Attorney General are directed to provide for enhanced consideration under the immigration laws for individuals from any country who express a fear of persecution upon return to their country related to that country's policy of forced abortion or coerced sterilization, as implemented by the Attorney General's regu-lation effective January 29, 1990.

Section 5. The Attorney General is directed to ensure that the Immigra-tion and Nationalization Service finalizes and makes public its position on the issue of training for individuals in F-1 visa status and on the issue of reinstatement into lawful nonimmigrant status of such PRC nationals who have withdrawn their applications for asylum.

Section 6. The Departments of Justice and State are directed to consider other steps to assist such PRC nationals in their efforts to utilize the pro-tections that I have extended pursuant to this order.

Section 7. This order shall be effective immediately.

George Bush
THE WHITE HOUSE
April 11, 1990

Our Interview Protocol

ID# _____

Interviewer _____

Location _____

Language of interview _____

Date _____

Questionnaire for Chinese Students and Scholars

February 17, 1993

All answers will be kept strictly confidential. You will be given a number to protect your identity.

The interview will take about an hour and 15 minutes.

---

1. What year were you born? 19____
2. What is your sex? _____
   (1) male
   (2) female
3. How good do you think your English is? _____
   (1) fluent
   (2) average
   (3) passable
   (4) poor
   (5) don't know
4. Which of the following choices best describes your family background? _____
   (1) high-ranking cadre
   (2) middle-ranking cadre (includes managers, bureaucrats)
   (3) worker
   (4) peasant
   (5) intellectual (job in a university)
   (6) business background

(7)　other (please specify) _____
(8)　don't know

5. What was your last position or job in China? _____

6. What was the highest level of education you attained in China? _____

_____
(1)　undergraduate
(2)　M.A.
(3)　Ph.D.
(4)　other (please specify) _____

7. In what year did you receive this degree? 19___

8. What was the location of your last job? _____

9. Which of the following best describes your work unit? _____
(1)　office in bureaucracy
(2)　university department
(3)　production unit
(4)　business unit or trading company
(5)　research lab in research institute or university
(6)　other (please specify) _____
(7)　don't know

10. How long had you been working before you left China? _____

11. How many academic books or articles did you publish before leaving China?
(1)　books:　　a. collectively _____; b. individually _____
(2)　articles:　a. collectively _____; b. individually _____

12. Did you receive any research grants before leaving China?

	Total number	Total amount
National level	_____	_____
Provincial and ministry level	_____	_____
City level	_____	_____
Contracts with production enterprises	_____	_____

13. Using the scale below, how would you describe your relationship with your unit's leader? _____
(1)　excellent
(2)　good
(3)　average
(4)　poor
(5)　bad
relationship with your immediate supervisor? _____
(1)　excellent

(2) good
(3) average
(4) poor
(5) bad
personal relationships (*renji guanxi*) in your work unit? _____
(1) excellent
(2) good
(3) average
(4) poor
(5) bad
opportunities for promotion? _____
(1) excellent
(2) good
(3) average
(4) poor
(5) bad

14. How would you evaluate the opportunities within your unit to develop your abilities (*fazhan qiantu*)? _____
(1) very good
(2) relatively good
(3) average
(4) very little
(5) not at all

15. Please explain why. _____

16. Overall, how satisfied were you with your job in China? _____
(1) very satisfied
(2) somewhat satisfied
(3) neither satisfied nor dissatisfied
(4) not very satisfied
(5) not satisfied at all

17. What was your salary when you left China? _____
(1)   was not earning any salary
(2)   under 50 yuan
(3)   50-60 yuan
(4)   60-75 yuan
(5)   75-100 yuan
(6)   100-120 yuan
(7)   120-150 yuan
(8)   150-200 yuan
(9)   200-250 yuan
(10) 250-300 yuan
(11) over 300 yuan

18. Please describe your housing in China: _____
    (1)   lived at home with my parents
    (2)   lived in a dormitory
    (3)   one-room apartment
    (4)   one bedroom, one sitting room
    (5)   two bedrooms, one sitting room
    (6)   three bedrooms, one sitting room
    (7)   four bedrooms, one sitting room or better
19. Before you left China, what did you think about your overall living conditions? _____
    (1)   very good
    (2)   good
    (3)   average
    (4)   not so good
    (5)   not good at all
20. Before you left China to come to the United States/Canada, what were your intentions about staying in this country? _____
    (1)   definitely planned to return to China after finishing your studies
    (2)   had planned to switch into a degree program, but still intended to return to China after getting the degree
    (3)   was undecided about returning; planned to stay a while and decide later
    (4)   intended to remain in the United States/Canada permanently even before you left China
21. Why did you have this view? _____
22. How many times had you been abroad before this time? _____
    (1)   just this time
    (2)   once before (dates: _____)
    (3)   twice before (dates: _____)
    (4)   more than twice (dates for the longest two trips: _____)
23. When did you arrive in the United States/Canada? _____
24. What were your original purposes for coming out? _____
    (1)   get an M.A.
    (2)   get a Ph.D.
    (3)   visiting scholar
    (4)   participate in a collaborative project
    (5)   attend a conference
    (6)   be with spouse
    (7)   other (please specify) _____
25. What was your immigration status at the time you came? _____

(1) F-1 (student) visa holder
(2) J-1 (exchange or visiting scholar) visa holder
(3) J-1 (student) visa holder
(4) H (temporary worker) visa holder
(5) B (tourist, visitor) visa holder
(6) G4 (international employee) visa holder
(7) permanent resident of the United States/Canada
(8) U.S./Canadian citizen
(9) other (please specify) _____

26. What is your immigration status now? _____
(1) F-1 (student) visa holder
(2) J-1 (exchange or visiting scholar) visa holder
(3) J-1 (student) visa holder
(4) H (temporary worker) visa holder
(5) B (tourist, visitor) visa holder
(6) G4 (international employee) visa holder
(7) permanent resident of the United States/Canada
(8) U.S./Canadian citizen
(9) others (please specify) _____

27. What was the length of the original program under which you came to the United States/Canada? _____
(1) less than 6 months
(2) six months to a year
(3) one year to eighteen months
(4) two years
(5) more than two years

28. When did you complete your original program? _____ (yr/mo)

29. Please indicate which agencies or parties provided tuition and/or living and travel expenses for you and what percentage of expenses that was.

	Tuition	Living	Travel	Other
Chinese government				
Your university in the United States/Canada				
International foundations				
Families and friends				
Self-support				

30. If you received funds from an international organization, what international foundation gave them to you? _____

31. What was your field of study when you arrived in the United

States/Canada? _____
(1) natural sciences
(2) applied sciences
(3) business or management
(4) applied social sciences (law, economics)
(5) social sciences
(6) humanities and fine arts
(7) other (please specify) _____

32. If you have changed your field since you came here, what is your new field? _____
(1) natural sciences
(2) applied sciences
(3) business or management
(4) applied social sciences (law, economics)
(5) social sciences
(6) humanities and fine arts
(7) other (please specify) _____

33. Why did you change your field? _____

34. Have you had any publications since leaving China?
(1) books: a. collectively _____; b. individually _____
(2) articles: a. collectively _____; b. individually _____

35. Did you apply for and receive any research funds in the United States/Canada? Please tell me what they were and for how much money.

Grant name	Amount of funds
_____	_____
_____	_____

36. What degree are you currently working for? _____
(1) undergraduate
(2) M.A. or equivalent
(3) Ph.D. or equivalent
(4) postdoctorate
(5) other (please specify) _____

37. If you are not a degree student, what is the nature of your studies/research? _____

38. If you have already graduated from school, what is your major source of income? _____
(1) full-time employment
(2) part-time employment
(3) spouse's income
(4) other (please specify) _____

39. What is you marital status? _____

(1) married
(2) single
(3) divorced
(4) widowed

40. How long have you been/were you married? _____

41. Is your spouse with you in the United States/Canada? _____
(1) yes
(2) no

42. If yes, what is your spouse's attitude about being here? _____
(1) very happy to be here
(2) happy to be here
(3) neither happy nor sad
(4) somewhat unhappy to be here
(5) very unhappy to be here
(6) hasn't been here long enough to have an opinion
(7) don't know what spouse thinks

43. If no, did you try to get him/her out? _____
(1) yes
(2) no

44. If yes, what happened? _____
    If no, what happened? _____

45. What does/did your spouse do in China? _____

46. What did/does your spouse do here in the United
    States/Canada? _____

47. Did your spouse support your coming to the United
    States/Canada? _____
(1) very supportive
(2) somewhat supportive
(3) neither supportive nor opposed
(4) somewhat opposed
(5) completely opposed

48. Why did he/she take that attitude? _____

49. What is your spouse's current view about your remaining in the
    United States/Canada? _____
(1) strongly wants you to stay
(2) wants you to stay
(3) does not care or is unsure
(4) wants you to go/come home
(5) strongly wants you to go/come home

50. Why does she/he have this view? _____

51. Do you have children? _____
(1) yes

(2)   no

52.   How old are they?
    (1)   one child (age: _____)
    (2)   two children (ages: _____)
    (3)   more (ages: _____)

53.   Are the children with you in the United States/Canada? _____
    (1)   yes
    (2)   no

54.   If no, are you planning to bring them here (or bring them out of China)? _____
    (1)   yes
    (2)   no

55.   What plans do you have for your children's public school education? _____
    (1)   study outside China
    (2)   study in China
    (3)   haven't thought about it at all

56.   What plans do you have for your children's college education?

    _____
    (1)   have them go to university outside China
    (2)   have them go to university in China
    (3)   don't care if they go to university
    (4)   haven't thought about it

57.   What are your parents' current views about your remaining in the United States/Canada? _____
    (1)   strongly want you to stay
    (2)   want you to stay
    (3)   do not care or are unsure
    (4)   want you to go/come home
    (5)   strongly want you to go/come home

58.   Why do they have this view? _____

59.   Does their view have any influence on your decision? _____
    (1)   a great deal of influence
    (2)   a certain degree of influence
    (3)   only a little influence
    (4)   no influence at all

60.   In what ways do you plan to help your family back in China?

    _____
    (1)   help bring them to the United States/Canada
    (2)   send them goods that are difficult to find in China
    (3)   give them financial support
    (4)   buy them a house

(5)   other (please specify) _____
61.   Are you already doing business with China? _____
    (1)   yes
    (2)   no
62.   If no, are you planning to do business with China? _____
    (1)   yes
    (2)   no
63.   If yes, what specific business are you doing or planning to do?
    (please tell us something about your current business activities)

    _____

64.   Describe your housing conditions here in the United
    States/Canada. _____
    (1)   studio
    (2)   one-bedroom apartment
    (3)   two-bedroom apartment
    (4)   room in shared house or apartment
    (5)   own your own house or condominium
    (6)   other (please specify) _____
65.   If you rent, what is your rent per month? $ _____
66.   If you own one or more apartments or houses, what is their
    total value? $ _____
67.   How do you evaluate your housing here in the United States?
    _____
    (1)   excellent
    (2)   good
    (3)   average
    (4)   rather poor
    (5)   very poor
68.   How do you compare your housing here to your housing back
    in China? _____
    (1)   much better
    (2)   a little better
    (3)   same
    (4)   a little worse
    (5)   much worse
69.   What is your total household income before taxes? _____
    (1) $0-$4,999
    (2) $5,000-$7,499
    (3) $7,500-$9,999
    (4) $10,000-$12,499
    (5) $12,500-$14,999
    (6) $15,000-$19,999

      (7) $20,000-$24,999
      (8) $25,000-$34,999
      (9) $35,000-50,000
      (10) above $50,000

70.   How would you evaluate your income here? _____
      (1)   excellent
      (2)   good
      (3)   average
      (4)   rather poor
      (5)   very poor

71.   How would you compare your income here to your income in China? _____
      (1)   much better
      (2)   a little better
      (3)   same
      (4)   a little worse
      (5)   much worse

72.   How would you describe your overall living standard here in the United States/Canada? _____
      (1)   excellent
      (2)   good
      (3)   average
      (4)   poor
      (5)   bad

73.   How do you compare your overall economic situation here to your economic situation in China? _____
      (1)   much better
      (2)   a little better
      (3)   same
      (4)   a little worse
      (5)   much worse

74.   In general, every society has its strengths and weaknesses. Here is a list. Please choose three positive things about the United States that are most important to you and rank them ("1" being highest ranking).
      (1)   political freedom _____
      (2)   job mobility _____
      (3)   good personal relations among people _____
      (4)   good interpersonal relations on the job _____
      (5)   lots of job choices or opportunity _____
      (6)   good working conditions _____
      (7)   higher standard of living _____

(8)   a better future for my children _____
(9)   other (please specify) _____
75.   Here is a list of some of the problems in U.S. society. Please choose the three most important factors and rank them ("1" being highest ranking).
(1)   pressure and speed of life too fast _____
(2)   poor living conditions _____
(3)   racism _____
(4)   crime and personal insecurity _____
(5)   poor interpersonal relations among people _____
(6)   missing family or friends _____
(7)   job insecurity _____
(8)   other (please specify) _____
76.   Please describe the social network that you have here in the United States/Canada. _____
(1)   almost totally Chinese
(2)   mostly with other Chinese
(3)   half of time with other Chinese, half with non-Chinese
(4)   mostly with non-Chinese
77.   What is your current attitude about returning to China? _____
(1)   definitely will go back and have made arrangements to do so
(2)   definitely will go back but don't know when
(3)   probably will go back and have kept up strong ties with China
(4)   probably will go back but have not kept up ties
(5)   not very likely to go back, but might go if things changed in China greatly
(6)   definitely will not go back
(7)   can't really say now
78.   If you chose 1, what are your specific plans? _____
79.   If you chose 3, please outline those contacts. _____
80.   If you chose 5, what kind of changes would have to occur for you to decide to go back? _____
81.   If you definitely are not returning, when did you make that decision? _____
82.   Have you returned to China in the past few years to see how things are there? _____
(1)   yes
(2)   no
83.   If yes, how did you feel about your visit? _____
(1)   very good

     (2)   good
     (3)   neither good nor bad
     (4)   somewhat bad
     (5)   quite bad

84.   Please describe your feelings in more detail. _____

85.   Did your visit affect your attitude about going back to China? _____

     (1)   increased my desire to go back greatly
     (2)   increased my interest to go back somewhat
     (3)   had no real impact on my attitude about returning
     (4)   made it less likely that I would go back
     (5)   convinced me that I definitely would not go back

86.   A number of reasons might motivate an individual to return to China. Here is a list of possible reasons why people might return to China. If you were to go back to China now, what would be the three most important reasons for you to return (please rank, "1" being highest)?
     (1)   patriotism _____
     (2)   family ties in China _____
     (3)   higher social status in China _____
     (4)   want to be involved in changing China _____
     (5)   better career opportunities in China than in the United States _____
     (6)   the new opportunities and situation that have emerged since Deng's "southern trip" _____
     (7)   better education for your children _____
     (8)   cultural comfort in China _____
     (9)   opportunity to make more money in China now than here in the United States/Canada _____

87.   Is there any reason I have not mentioned that you think is important in making people go back to China? _____

88.   Here is a list of reasons why people might not return to China. If you were to decide now not to go back, what would be the three most important factors affecting your decision (please rank, "1" being highest)?
     (1)   lack of political stability _____
     (2)   lack of political freedom _____
     (3)   fear of being arrested _____
     (4)   lack of opportunities to change jobs in China _____
     (5)   lack of opportunity for career advancement in China _____

     (6)   poor work environment in China _____

(7) lack of equipment for your research or work _____
(8) living standard in China too low _____
(9) family here does not want to return _____
(10) difficulty in getting out the first time _____
(11) returnees looked on as failures _____
(12) fear of not being able to get out a second time _____
(13) better opportunity here for children's future _____
(14) difficulty for children to compete with children of similar age back in China _____
(15) lack of suitable jobs given your education and training _____
(16) lack of contact or exchanges with international scholars in your field _____

89. Is there any reason I have not mentioned that is important? _____

90. Did your family suffer during the Cultural Revolution? _____
(1) yes
(2) no

91. How important was this to your decision not to go back? ____
(1) very important
(2) somewhat important
(3) not very important
(4) not important at all
(5) difficult to say

92. What was the effect of June 4, 1989, on your decision whether or not to stay in the United States/Canada? _____
(1) very important
(2) somewhat important
(3) not very important
(4) not important at all
(5) difficult to say

93. Why? _____

94. How many of your friends and colleagues have returned to China within the last six years to live permanently? _____

95. Why did they go back? _____

96. Were most of them who have returned _____
(1) very satisfied
(2) somewhat satisfied
(3) neither satisfied nor dissatisfied
(4) somewhat dissatisfied
(5) very dissatisfied

97. Recently the Chinese government has made some new policies

about letting returned scholars go back and forth freely. Have you heard about these policies?
  (1) yes
  (2) no

98. Do you believe that they will keep this promise? _____
  (1) completely trust
  (2) trust somewhat
  (3) uncertain
  (4) somewhat mistrust
  (5) strongly mistrust

99. What do you think about these changes? _____
  (1) very significant
  (2) somewhat significant
  (3) not very significant
  (4) of no significance at all
  (5) hard to say

100. Why? _____

101. What policies do you think the government should introduce that would have a big impact on people's decisions about returning? _____

102. How often do you have contact with your home unit? _____
  (1) never had contact with my home unit
  (2) now have no contact with my home unit
  (3) once a year
  (4) three times a year
  (5) six times a year
  (6) didn't have a home unit to keep in touch with
  (7) other (please specify) _____

103. What kind of contacts do you have with them? (for yes, mark 1; for no, mark 2)
  (1) helped colleagues come to study or as visiting scholars

  _____
  (2) helped bring over a delegation from your unit _____
  (3) shared information with colleagues about conditions or research in United States/Canada _____
  (4) exchanged data, books, or technology with home unit in China _____
  (5) gave home unit financial support _____
  (6) went back to unit to give a lecture _____
  (7) other (please specify) _____

104. What does your unit think about your returning to China?

_____

(1)   strongly want me to return
(2)   would be pleased if I return
(3)   don't care either way if I return or not
(4)   don't really want me to come back
(5)   don't know if they want me to come back

105. If you are thinking of going back, will you go back to your
original unit? _____
(1)   certainly will go back to my original unit
(2)   possibly will go back to my original unit
(3)   uncertain
(4)   probably won't go back to my original unit
(5)   certainly won't go back to my original unit

Table 1. Responses to Question 77:
"What Is Your Current Attitude about Returning to China?"

Category	Description	Frequency	Percent
1	Definitely returning and have made plans to do so	22	8.3
2	Definitely returning but don't know when	66	24.4
3	Probably returning and have strong ties with China	53	19.9
4	Can't really say now (ambivalent)	53	19.9
5	Probably will return but have not kept up ties	26	9.8
6	Not very likely to return but might if things in China changed greatly	27	10.2
7	Definitely will not go back	20	7.5
TOTAL		267*	100

* missing data = 6

Figure 4. Responses to Question 77

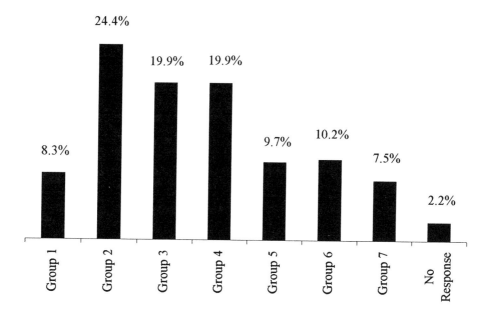

Table 2. Why a Person Might Return to China: Responses to Question 86

Choices	Rank as 1st choice	Frequency	Percent	Rank as 2d choice	Rank as 3d choice	Combined rank*
1 Patriotism	3	44	17.3	5	4	4
2 Family ties in China	4	39	15.4	1	2	3
3 Higher social status in China	1	66	26.0	2	3	1
4 Want to be involved in Chinese reform	6	15	5.9	4	6	6
5 Better career opportunities in China	2	52	20.5	3	4	2
6 Positive effects of Deng's "trip south"	7	6	2.4	8	6	9
7 Better education for children	8	4	1.6	6	5	8
8 Cultural comfort in China	5	22	8.7	4	1	5
9 Can make more money in China than U.S./Canada	7	6	2.4	7	7	7
TOTAL	n/a	254	100.0**	n/a	n/a	n/a

* Determined according to the sum of 1st, 2d, and 3d choices (1st choice given a value of 5, 2d choice a value of 3, 3d choice a value of 1).

** The total was 254 because we had 19 cases of missing data. We calculated "valid percentages" for those 254 cases.

Table 3. Why a Person Might Not Return to China: Responses to Question 88

Choices	Rank as 1st choice	Frequency	Percent	Rank as 2d choice	Rank as 3d choice	Combined rank *
1 Lack of political stability	1	76	30.3	5	7	1
2 Lack of political freedom	2	31	12.4	2	6	2
3 Fear of being arrested	11	3	1.2	15	11	15
4 Lack of opportunities to change jobs in China	6	15	6.0	6	4	6
5 Lack of opportunity for career advancement in China	3	29	11.6	3	2	3
6 Poor work environment in China	4	21	8.4	1	3	4
7 Lack of modern equipment for your research or work	7	14	5.6	9	3	7
8 Living standard in China too low	5	19	7.6	4	8	5
9 Family here does not want to return	12	2	0.8	12	12	14
10 Difficulty in getting out the first time	9	8	3.2	10	5	10
11 People look on people who have returned as if they have failed	10	6	2.4	13	10	13
12 Fear of not being able to get out a second time	9	8	3.2	7	10	9
13 Better opportunity here for children's future	8	9	3.6	8	9	8
14 Difficulty competing with children of similar age back in China	13	1	0.4	14	10	16
15 Lack of suitable jobs given your education and training	11	3	1.3	12	6	12
16 Lack of contact or exchanges with international scholars in your field	10	6	2.4	11	2	11
TOTAL	n/a	251	100**	n/a	n/a	n/a

* Determined according to the sum of 1st, 2d, and 3d choices (1st choice given a value of 5, 2d choice a value of 3, 3d choice a value of 1).

** We calculated "valid percentages" based on the 251 people who responded. We had 22 cases of missing data.

Table 4. Positive Things about United States: Responses to Question 74

Choices	Rank as 1st choice	Frequency	Percent	Rank as 2d choice	Rank as 3d choice	Combined rank*
1 Political freedom	1	103	38.6	5	3	1
2 Job mobility	4	27	10.1	4	5	5
3 Good personal relations among people	6	10	3.7	7	8	7
4 Good interpersonal relations on the job	9	3	1.1	8	7	9
5 Lots of job choices or opportunity	2	52	19.5	1	4	2
6 Good working conditions	3	36	13.5	3	2	3
7 Higher standard of living	5	21	7.9	2	1	4
8 A better future for my children	7	9	3.4	6	6	6
9 Other	8	6	2.2	9	9	8
TOTAL	n/a	267	100.0**	n/a	n/a	n/a

* Determined according to the sum of 1st, 2d, and 3d choices (1st choice given a value of 5, 2d choice a value of 3, 3d choice a value of 1).

** We calculated the "valid percentages" based on 267 cases. We had 6 cases of missing data.

Table 5. Problems in American Society: Responses to Question 75

Choices	Rank as 1st choice	Frequency	Percent	Rank as 2d choice	Rank as 3d choice	Combined rank*
1 Pressure and speed of life is too fast	1	83	31.1	4	4	1
2 Poor living conditions	7	3	1.1	7	8	8
3 Racism	4	26	9.7	3	2	4
4 Crime and personal insecurity	2	78	29.2	2	6	2
5 Poor interpersonal relations among people	6	11	4.1	6	3	6
6 Missing family or friends	5	18	6.7	5	5	5
7 Job insecurity	3	46	17.2	1	1	3
8 Other	8	2	0.7	8	9	7
TOTAL	n/a	267	100.0**	n/a	n/a	n/a

* Determined according to the sum of 1st, 2d, and 3d choices (1st choice given a value of 5, 2d choice a value of 3, 3d choice a value of 1).

** We calculated the "valid percentages" based on 267 cases. We had 6 cases of missing data.

Table 6. Why a Person Might Return to China: Responses to Question 86 for Those "Leaning toward Returning" (Answering 1-3 on Question 77)

Choices	Rank as 1st choice	Frequency	Percent	Rank as 2d choice	Rank as 3d choice	Combined rank*
1 Patriotism	2	27	20.6	5	3	4
2 Family ties in China	4	17	13.0	1	3	3
3 Higher social status in China	1	35	26.7	4	2	1
4 Want to be involved in Chinese reform	5	11	8.4	2	6	6
5 Better career opportunities in China	3	25	19.1	3	4	2
6 Positive effects of Deng's "trip south"	7	1	0.8	7	7	9
7 Better education for children	7	1	0.8	6	5	8
8 Cultural comfort in China	5	11	8.4	2	1	5
9 Can make more money in China than U.S./Canada	6	3	2.3	7	8	7
TOTAL	n/a	131	100.0**	n/a	n/a	n/a

* Determined according to the sum of 1st, 2d, and 3d choices (1st choice given a value of 5, 2d choice a value of 3, 3d choice a value of 1.

** We calculated the "valid percentage" based on 131 cases. We had 10 cases of missing data, as 141 people fell into categories 1-3.

Table 7. Why a Person Might Not Return to China: First Choices on Question 88 for Those "Leaning toward Remaining in U.S." (Answering 5-7 on Question 77)

Choices	Rank as 1st choice	Frequency	Percent	Rank as 2d choice	Rank as 3d choice	Combined rank*
1 Lack of political stability	1	21	30.4	5	7	1
2 Lack of political freedom	2	10	14.5	1	6	2
3 Fear of being arrested	8	1	1.4	not chosen	5	14
4 Lack of opportunities to change jobs in China	5	4	5.8	2	2	4
5 Lack of opportunity for career advancement in China	3	8	11.6	4	4	3
6 Poor work environment in China	4	6	8.7	4	3	4
7 Lack of modern equipment for your research or work	6	3	4.3	8	8	8
8 Living standard in China too low	5	4	5.8	5	1	5
9 Family here does not want to return	8	1	1.4	7	8	11
10 Difficulty in getting out the first time	7	2	2.9	9	3	9
11 People look on people who have returned as if they have failed	7	2	2.9	not chosen	6	12
12 Fear of not being able to get out a second time	6	3	4.3	3	8	7
13 Better opportunity here for children's future	5	4	5.8	5	3	6
14 Difficulty competing with children of similar age back in China	not chosen	0	0	not chosen	not chosen	15
15 Lack of suitable jobs given your education and training	not chosen	0	0	6	5	10
16 Lack of contact or exchanges with international scholars in your field	not chosen	0	0	8	4	13
TOTAL	n/a	69	100.0**	n/a	n/a	n/a

* Determined according to the sum of 1st, 2d, and 3d choices (1st choice given a value of 5, 2d choice a value of 3, 3d choice a value of 1).

** We calculated the "valid percentages" based on 69 cases. We had 4 cases of missing data, as 73 people fell into categories 5-7.

Table 8. Results of the Logistic Analysis of Key Factors Explaining
Views about Returning: with Children, with Education Variable, Version 2

Variable		Parameter estimate	Standard errors of the estimate	Probability chi-square	Standardized estimate
N2	Sex	1.5113	0.7566	0.0458**	0.394037
N10	How long they worked before they left China	-0.0913	0.0695	0.1889	-0.382569
N20	What their original intentions were about staying/leaving before coming to U.S.	-1.6017	0.4176	0.0001**	-0.909213
N26	Current visa status	-1.1481	0.6657	0.0846*	-0.442821
N55	Plans for their children's public school education	0.8925	0.8659	0.3027	0.244234
N56	Plans for their children's college education	-0.2449	0.7483	0.7435	-0.066338
N67	How they evaluate their housing in the U.S.	-0.2925	0.5246	0.5771	-0.136869
N68	How they compare U.S. housing to housing in China	1.5075	0.4419	0.0006**	1.203285
N69	Household income	-0.0578	0.1717	0.7363	-0.087766
N73	How they compare overall economic situation now to that in China	0.00918	0.4044	0.9819	0.005279
N98	Trust of new policies regarding free travel back to U.S. after returning to China	-0.5729	0.3773	0.1289	-0.356015
N102	Degree of contact with home unit	0.1645	0.3208	0.6081	0.115311
N104	Unit's opinion about their return to China	-0.5816	0.2987	0.0515*	-0.372891
Other	Arrival before or after April 1990	-1.6847	0.013	0.0963*	-0.447125
Other	Combined political variable	0.2883	0.1506	0.0556*	0.391918

Criterion: -2 LOG L
Chi-square for covariates: 91.445 with 15 DF ($P = .0001$)
* Indicates a significant relationship
** Indicates a highly significant relationship

Table 9. Results of the Logistic Analysis of Key Factors Explaining Views about Returning: with Children, no Education Variable, Version 2

Variable		Parameter estimate	Standard errors of the estimate	Probability chi-square	Standardized estimate
N2	Sex	1.3051	0.5785	0.0241**	0.329188
N10	How long they worked before they left China	-0.0583	0.0497	0.2407	-0.237538
N20	What their original intentions were about staying/leaving before coming to U.S.	-1.2821	0.3151	0.0001**	-0.699179
N26	Current visa status	-1.2647	0.4923	0.0102**	-0.475395
N67	How they evaluate their housing in the U.S.	-0.568	0.4156	0.1713	-0.264422
N68	How they compare U.S. housing to housing in China	1.0295	0.3184	0.0012**	0.769709
N69	Household income	-0.0491	0.1208	0.6847	-0.071369
N73	How they compare overall economic situation now to that in China	0.1852	0.3109	0.5515	0.102882
N98	Trust of new policies regarding free travel back to U.S. after returning to China	-0.6754	0.3021	0.0253**	-0.386327
N102	Degree of contact with home unit	0.1963	0.2342	0.4019	0.131826
N104	Unit's opinion about their return to China	-0.1087	0.2001	0.5867	-0.071381
Other	Arrival before or after April 1990	-1.3445	0.7059	0.0568*	-0.366649
Other	Combined political variable	0.1928	0.1095	0.0783*	0.267561

Criterion: -2 LOG L
Chi-square for covariates: 101.480 with 13 DF (P=0.0001)
Score: 65.979 with 13 DF (P=.0001)
    * Indicates a significant relationship
  ** Indicates a highly significant relationship

Table 10. Results of the Logistic Analysis of Key Factors Explaining Views about Returning: no Children, Version 2

Variable		Parameter estimate	Standard errors of the estimate	Probability chi-square	Standardized estimate
N2	Sex	0.8236	0.5709	0.1491	0.215566
N10	How long they worked before they left China	0.1348	0.063	0.0322**	0.399826
N20	What their original intentions were about staying/leaving before coming to U.S.	-0.5619	0.3487	0.1071	-0.270171
N26	Current visa status	1.8844	0.7688	0.0142**	0.410988
N67	How they evaluate their housing in the U.S.	0.2506	0.3905	0.5211	0.124521
N68	How they compare U.S. housing to housing in China	-0.3584	0.3549	0.3125	-0.213499
N69	Household income	-0.3676	0.1358	0.0068**	-0.499966
N73	How they compare overall economic situation now to that in China	0.6713	0.3314	0.0428**	0.35407
N98	Trust of new policies regarding free travel back to U.S. after returning to China	-0.6099	0.3604	0.0906*	-0.257547
N102	Degree of contact with home unit	0.0491	0.2492	0.8439	0.031118
N104	Unit's opinion about their return to China	0.1884	0.1893	0.3198	0.141482
Other	Arrival before or after April 1990	-0.4735	0.7484	0.527	-0.115853
Other	Combined political variable	-0.1895	0.1184	0.1093	-0.254662

Criterion: -2 LOG L
Chi-square for covariates: 30.650 with 13 DF (P=0.0038)
Score: 24.738 with 13 DF (P=.0250)
 * Indicates a significant relationship
 ** Indicates a highly significant relationship

Table 11: Results of the Logistic Analysis of Key Factors Explaining Views about Returning: with Children, no Education Variable, Version 1

Variable		Parameter estimate	Standard errors of the estimate	Probability chi-square	Standardized estimate
N2	Sex	-0.8734	0.4221	0.0385**	-0.220292
N10	How long they worked before they left China	-0.0351	0.0285	0.2194	-0.142511
N20	What their original intentions were about staying/leaving before coming to U.S.	-0.3349	0.2161	0.1211	-0.182625
N26	Current visa status	0.9342	0.3729	0.0122**	0.351168
N67	How they evaluate their housing in the U.S.	0.4239	0.2911	0.1454	0.197331
N68	How they compare U.S. housing to housing in China	-0.1781	0.2006	0.3747	-0.133146
N69	Household income	-0.1796	0.0875	0.0401**	-0.261368
N73	How they compare overall economic situation now to that in China	0.2846	0.2219	0.1997	0.158107
N98	Trust of new policies regarding free travel back to U.S. after returning to China	-0.2006	0.2184	0.3586	-0.114715
N102	Degree of contact with home unit	0.2931	0.1725	0.0894*	0.196807
N104	Unit's opinion about their return to China	0.1294	0.1542	0.4013	0.084953
Other	Arrival before or after April 1990	-1.1074	0.5077	0.0292**	-0.301975
Other	Combined political variable	0.0501	0.0833	0.5478	0.069455

Criterion: -2 LOG L
Chi-square for covariates: 28.689 with 13 DF (P =0.0072)
Score: 24.463 with 13 DF (P =.0072)
* Indicates a significant relationship
** Indicates a highly significant relationship

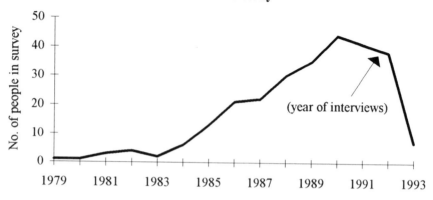

Figure 1. Date of Arrival in U.S. of People Interviewed for this Study

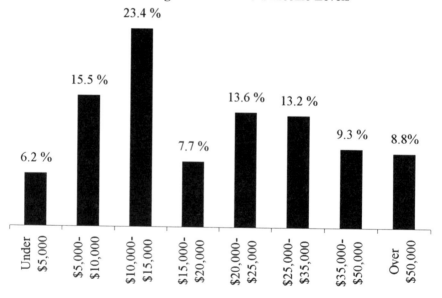

Figure 2. Household Income Levels

Figure 3. Quality of Housing in the U.S.

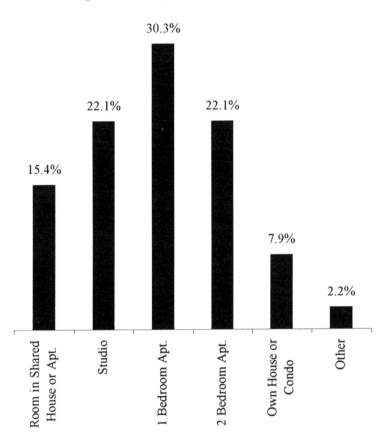

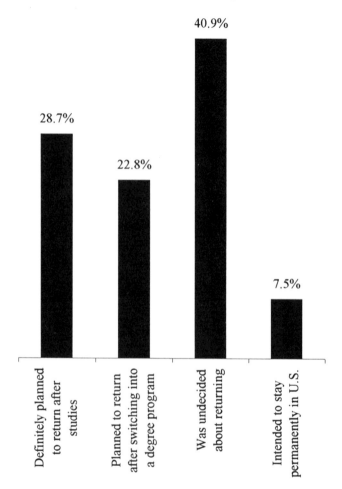

Figure 5. Intentions about Staying in the U.S. before Leaving China

Figure 6. Parents' Views on Staying/Returning

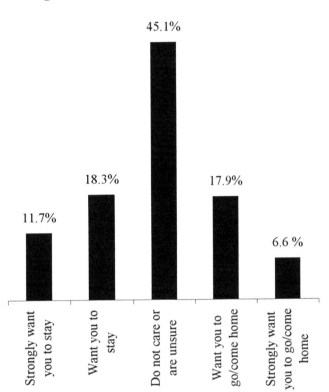

Figure 7. Effect of June 4 on Decision to Stay/Return

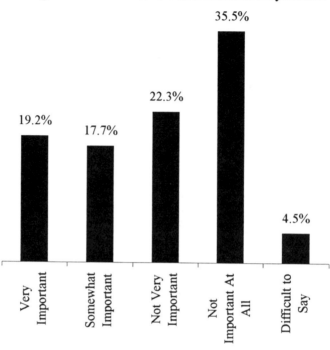

**Figure 8. Trust in New PRC Policies about Freedom
to Study Abroad after Returning (*Lai qu ziyou*)**

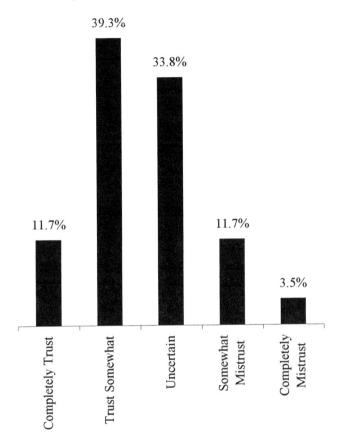

INSTITUTE OF EAST ASIAN STUDIES PUBLICATIONS SERIES

CHINA RESEARCH MONOGRAPHS (CRM)

6. David D. Barrett. *Dixie Mission: The U.S. Army Observer Group in Yenan, 1944,* 1970
17. Frederic Wakeman, Jr., ed. *Ming and Qing Historical Studies in the People's Republic of China,* 1981
21. James H. Cole. *The People Versus the Taipings: Bao Lisheng's "Righteous Army of Dongan,"* 1981
24. Pao-min Chang. *Beijing, Hanoi, and the Overseas Chinese,* 1982
27. John N. Hart. *The Making of an Army "Old China Hand": A Memoir of Colonel David D. Barrett,* 1985
28. Steven A. Leibo. *Transferring Technology to China: Prosper Giquel and the Self-strengthening Movement,* 1985
29. David Bachman. *Chen Yun and the Chinese Political System,* 1985
30. Maria Hsia Chang. *The Chinese Blue Shirt Society: Fascism and Developmental Nationalism,* 1985
31. Robert Y. Eng. *Economic Imperialism in China: Silk Production and Exports, 1861–1932,* 1986
33. Yue Daiyun. *Intellectuals in Chinese Fiction,* 1988
34. Constance Squires Meaney. *Stability and the Industrial Elite in China and the Soviet Union,* 1988
35. Yitzhak Shichor. *East Wind over Arabia: Origins and Implications of the Sino-Saudi Missile Deal,* 1989
36. Suzanne Pepper. *China's Education Reform in the 1980s: Policies, Issues, and Historical Perspectives,* 1990
sp. Phyllis Wang and Donald A. Gibbs, eds. *Readers' Guide to China's Literary Gazette, 1949–1979,* 1990
38. James C. Shih. *Chinese Rural Society in Transition: A Case Study of the Lake Tai Area, 1368–1800,* 1992
39. Anne Gilks. *The Breakdown of the Sino-Vietnamese Alliance, 1970–1979,* 1992
sp. Theodore Han and John Li. *Tiananmen Square Spring 1989: A Chronology of the Chinese Democracy Movement,* 1992
40. Frederic Wakeman, Jr., and Wen-hsin Yeh, eds. *Shanghai Sojourners,* 1992
41. Michael Schoenhals. *Doing Things with Words in Chinese Politics: Five Studies,* 1992
sp. Kaidi Zhan. *The Strategies of Politeness in the Chinese Language,* 1992
42. Barry C. Keenan. *Imperial China's Last Classical Academies: Social Change in the Lower Yangzi, 1864–1911,* 1994
43. Ole Bruun. *Business and Bureaucracy in a Chinese City: An Ethnography of Private Business Households in Contemporary China,* 1993
44. Wei Li. *The Chinese Staff System: A Mechanism for Bureaucratic Control and Integration,* 1994
47. David Zweig and Chen Changgui. *China's Brain Drain to the United States: Views of Overseas Chinese Students and Scholars in the 1990s,* 1995

KOREA RESEARCH MONOGRAPHS (KRM)

9. Helen Hardacre. *The Religion of Japan's Korean Minority: The Preservation of Ethnic Identity,* 1985
10. Fred C. Bohm and Robert R. Swartout, Jr., eds. *Naval Surgeon in Yi Korea: The Journal of George W. Woods,* 1984
13. Vipan Chandra. *Imperialism, Resistance, and Reform in Late Nineteenth-Century Korea: Enlightenment and the Independence Club,* 1988
14. Seok Choong Song. *Explorations in Korean Syntax and Semantics,* 1988
15. Robert A. Scalapino and Dalchoong Kim, eds. *Asian Communism: Continuity and Transition,* 1988